Drive and Stroll i

G000095953

Kent

Michael Easterbrook

COUNTRYSIDE BOOKS
NEWBURY BERKSHIRE

First published 2005
© Michael Easterbrook, 2005

COUNTRYSIDE BOOKS
3 Catherine Road
Newbury, Berkshire

To view our complete range of books,
please visit us at
www.countrysidebooks.co.uk

ISBN 1 85306 906 X

Photographs by the author

Designed by Peter Davies, Nautilus Design
Produced through MRM Associates Ltd., Reading
Printed by Arrowsmith, Bristol

Contents

AREA MAP SHOWING LOCATIONS OF THE WALKS

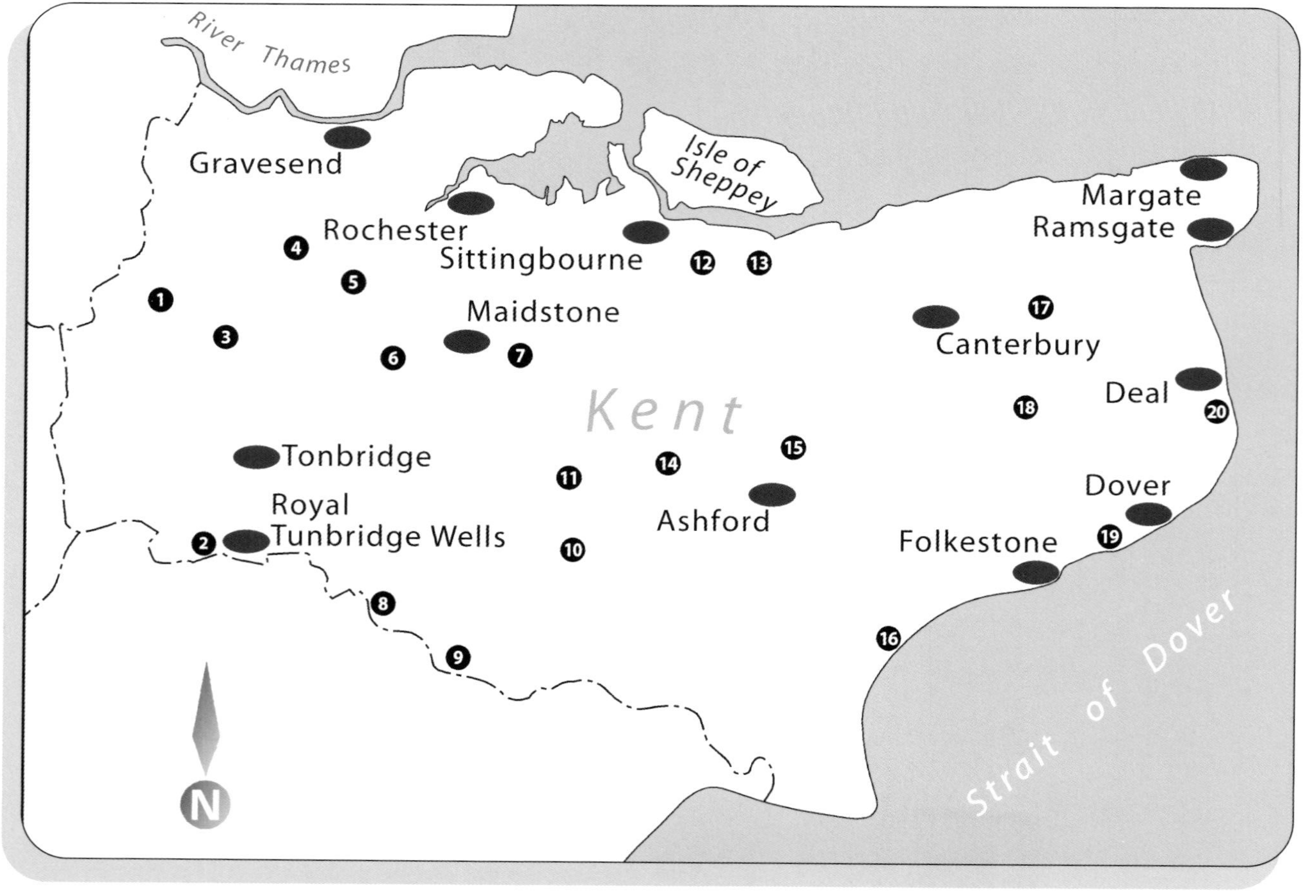

River Thames
Gravesend
Rochester
Sittingbourne
Isle of Sheppey
Maidstone
Margate
Ramsgate
Canterbury
Deal
Kent
Tonbridge
Royal Tunbridge Wells
Ashford
Dover
Folkestone
Strait of Dover
N
1
2
3
4
5
6
7
8
9
10
11
12
13
14
15
16
17
18
19
20

Contents

Publisher's Note

We hope that you obtain considerable enjoyment from this book; great care has been taken in its preparation. Although at the time of publication all routes followed public rights of way or permitted paths, diversion orders can be made and permissions withdrawn.

We cannot, of course, be held responsible for such diversion orders and any inaccuracies in the text which result from these or any other changes to the routes nor any damage which might result from walkers trespassing on private property. We are anxious though that all details covering the walks are kept up to date and would therefore welcome information from readers which would be relevant to future editions.

The simple sketch maps that accompany the walks in this book are based on notes made by the author whilst checking the routes on the ground. They are designed to show you how to reach the start and to point out the main features of the overall circuit, and they contain a progression of numbers that relate to the paragraphs of the text. However, for the benefit of a proper map, we do recommend that you purchase the relevant Ordnance Survey sheet covering your walk. The Ordnance Survey maps are widely available, especially through booksellers and local newsagents.

Introduction

Despite the pressure on its land as a result of its position in the south-east corner of England, Kent still has some wonderful countryside for walking and a large network of public footpaths. The walks in this book use a mixture of these field paths with quiet lanes to provide circular walks of 2 to 6 miles. They are spread throughout Kent, providing the opportunity to sample the varied landscapes of the county, from the rolling hills of the North Downs and the high Greensand Ridge to Wealden woods, the flatness of Romney Marsh, and bracing seaside promenades.

These different types of environment provide habitats for a range of wildlife, including colourful flowers and butterflies of the chalk downland, fantastic displays of bluebells and other spring flowers in the woods, and waders, wildfowl and seabirds on the river estuaries and seashore.

Kent is also rich in history, and these walks reveal ancient churches and manor houses, old windmills and watermills, medieval timbered houses, and fortifications ranging from a castle built by Henry VIII to Martello towers erected in Napoleonic times. You may also see miniature steam trains chugging across the marshland, restored sailing barges, yachts and pleasure boats on rivers and creeks, and ferries and other boats in the English Channel.

Although sketch maps are provided, with numbered points that correspond to the route description in the text, it is wise to have the appropriate Ordnance Survey Explorer map with you. Some sections of the walks can be muddy, especially after wet weather, so do wear appropriate footwear. Details are given of places to park, often in public car parks, but where the pub suggested as a source of refreshment is on or close to the route of the walk it may be possible to park there if eating at the establishment, but do ask the landlord's permission first. Many of the walks are accessible by public transport and where this is feasible, details are given. Details of timetables are available from National Rail Enquiries (08457 484950) or Traveline (0870 6082608).

I hope you enjoy doing the walks and discover more aspects of Kent, while getting some healthy exercise.

Michael Easterbrook

Acknowledgements

I would like to thank Jolene, Cheryl, Craig and Val Easterbrook, Mike Lyth, Roy and Chris Murray, and Tony Roberts for their company on various walks.

1 Otford

The Darent Valley, near Otford

The Walk 3 miles
Terrain Undulating, with one steep climb and descent
Map OS Explorer 147 Sevenoaks and Tonbridge (GR 526594)

How to get there

Otford is on the A225, some 3 miles north of Sevenoaks. Turn off the A225 at the roundabout with the duckpond to go along the main street. **Parking** In the public car park on the right of the main street. **Public transport** Otford railway station is on the route.

Drive and Stroll

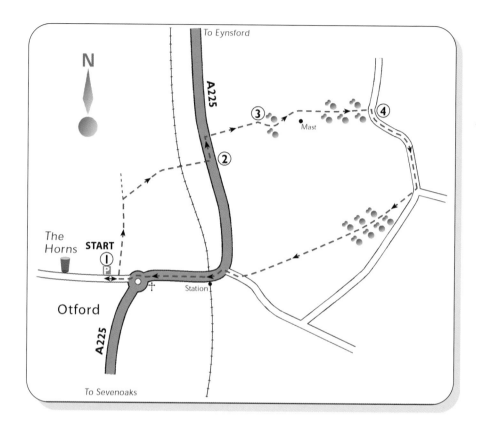

Introduction

This is one of the most strenuous walks in the book, involving quite a steep climb and descent. However, from the top of the Downs you are rewarded with wonderful views over the Darent Valley. You will also get the chance to admire at close quarters the rich flora of the chalk downland, including some lovely orchids. There are many colourful butterflies and day-flying moths in summer. The route continues on an ancient trackway through a wood; then goes along a lane before following the North Downs Way back to Otford, with more fine views. Back in the village, there are historic houses, including a former bishop's palace, and an ancient church to see, not to mention a listed duckpond.

The Horns

On the main street in Otford, the pretty tile-hung pub called the Horns has a hidden timber-framed structure dating back to the 16th/17th century, when it was divided into three cottages. The attractive dining areas feature these timbers, and the windows at the front look out on a lovely medieval house opposite. The extensive menu includes smoked salmon and prawns, rib of beef, and specials such as skate fillets and asparagus. Lighter meals such as omelettes and ploughman's are also available, plus sandwiches and a choice of ales. Telephone: 01959 522604.

There are also several other pubs and a café and tearoom in Otford.

THE WALK

Go out of the car park entrance and turn left for 150 yards; then, just past the **Forge** restaurant, go left on a track. (From the station turn left alongside the road that crosses the railway to reach the village pond and then continue straight on to reach the track in front of the Forge.) Follow this track past the truncated remains of a former oast house and, later, barns and animal sheds; then, 100 yards past these, go right up concrete steps to a kissing gate. Go diagonally left across the field towards the downs, aiming for the left corner of a fence and hedge at the far end. At the corner of the fence keep ahead for 30 yards to cross a busy railway line with great care and then continue on a path between garden fences to a road.

Cross and turn left alongside the road, taking care as the verge is narrow. After 300 yards go right at a stile, just past a white house called Wayside, to cross a field. In summer this meadow is colourful with flowers such as marjoram, red clover and thistles, and these attract clouds of meadow brown, gatekeeper and skipper butterflies. From the next stile continue straight ahead up the slope, now more steeply, to another stile, and ahead between wire fences.

While getting your breath, look back for a glorious view over the Darent Valley. The downland slopes here are rich in wild flowers, including pyramidal orchids, knapweed, milkwort and scabious, and you may see red and black burnet moths, common and chalkhill blue butterflies and even the rare dark green fritillary butterfly, which, despite its name, is orange and black.

As you reach the top of the hill there is a welcome seat.

Facing the seat, continue to the right of it and walk uphill into trees at a marker post. Keep on the main path where another goes off left, to reach a kissing gate after 80 yards and

Otford's medieval hall house

emerge from the trees. Walk ahead along the top of a ridge, with more fine views on the right across the valley to **Sevenoaks**, and a profusion of wild flowers in the turf. After 100 yards, turn left at a marker post to cross a stile next to a metal gate and walk under yew and beech trees to a stile to the left of a mast. Continue along the left edge of a field to a stile by a wooden gate; then keep straight ahead on a track into trees, ignoring a permissive path to the left. The path you are following is an ancient trackway and goes through a wood of sweet chestnut and other trees, with displays of bluebells in spring, to reach a stile to the left of a metal gate to a road, next to the drive to **Stursoon Farm**.

Turn right along the lane and follow it for ½ mile. Just before it reaches a T-junction the lane forks; take the right fork and then, after 20 yards, go right over a stile by a metal gate, to follow the **North Downs Way** long-distance footpath back to **Otford**. Go along the left edge of a long field; then ahead into trees, keeping on the main track under tall beech and ash trees, and then through scrubby blackthorn. There are steps in places as you go quite steeply downhill, with views over **Otford**, and finally between garden fences to a road. Cross with care to the path alongside the road. Turn right to a T-junction and then left to pass the railway station. Continue alongside the road until a road junction is reached, with the village pond in the centre, and keep straight ahead to return to the car park, with the **Horns pub** further along the street. To view the 11th-century church and the remains of the bishop's palace, go left at the pond.

Places of Interest Nearby

Lullingstone Castle, reached from the A225 north of Otford, is a Tudor manor house with an impressive 16th-century gatehouse. Telephone: 01322 862114.

Lullingstone Roman Villa (English Heritage) has the remains of several rooms, including the bathhouse, and some fine mosaics, all preserved under cover. Telephone: 01322 863467.

2 Langton Green

Ashurst Place

The Walk 3¾ miles
Terrain Undulating with one steepish climb
Map OS Explorer 147 Sevenoaks and Tonbridge (GR 543392)

How to get there

Langton Green is on the A264, 2 miles west of Tunbridge Wells. Travelling westwards, turn right by the Hare pub at the west end of the village. **Parking** There is limited parking alongside the green and there is a car park at the recreation ground (GR 544396). **Public transport** Langton Green is served by buses from Tunbridge Wells.

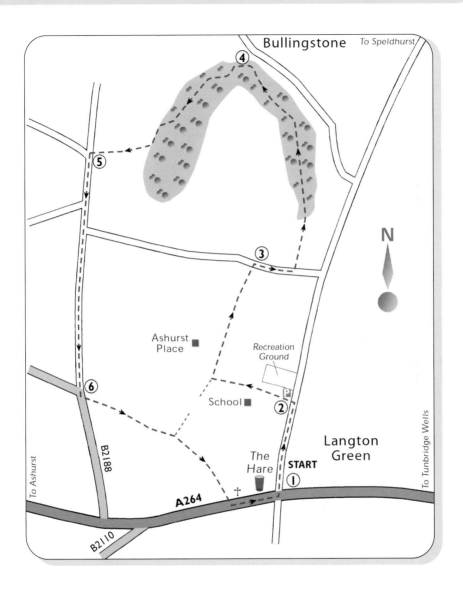

Drive and Stroll

Introduction

On the outskirts of Tunbridge Wells, this walk starts near a picturesque green with a manor house and a sandstone church that contains works by famous Pre-Raphaelite artists. The route passes grand 19th-century houses with fine specimen trees in the grounds and then follows field paths before entering ancient woodland. Here there are displays of bluebells and other flowers in spring, while in the deep, stream-cut clefts there is rather primeval-looking vegetation of ferns, horsetails and mosses flourishing in the damp conditions. The walk then continues along a quiet lane with tall hedges, before crossing fields to return to Langton Green and its inn.

The Hare

This pub is pleasantly situated by the green at Langton Green. It is spacious inside, with several nicely furnished rooms, and serves a very wide and imaginative choice of meals. The menu changes frequently, but typical examples are medallions of pork with pancetta and black pudding with a celeriac sauce, and baked whole trout with new potatoes and lime and caper hollandaise. There are also tempting desserts, vegetarian meals, ploughman's and sandwiches. Some outdoor seating is available. Telephone: 01892 862419.

THE WALK

If starting alongside the green, near the **Hare** pub, continue beside the road passing the green and bending right. Where the pavement ends by large houses named Stonewall and Searles, cross to the opposite pavement for 80 yards and then turn left at the sign for the recreation ground and car park.

Take the tarmac footpath that runs alongside the car park and past the sports pavilion. Where the path bends left, go ahead but slightly diagonally left across grass to a path between a children's playground and school grounds. Continue through a metal stile and along the left edge of a field to reach a wire fence.

*Beyond it, lie the grounds of **Ashurst Place**, containing lime trees with massive trunks. The house dates from the 1860s.*

Turn right in front of the fence to go on a wide grassy track, soon with fences on both sides. Go through two kissing gates and straight across a small field. Cross a tarmac drive leading to **Shirley Hall**, a large white house built in the early 19th century, which lies behind trees to the left. Go straight over another field to a marker post. Continue through trees for 15 yards to a kissing gate and then slightly diagonally right across a field to a gate in the far right corner, leading to a lane.

Turn right along the lane and later ignore a footpath sign on the right, but shortly after go left at the next sign, just past an oak tree, and cross a stile. Go through trees, over a plank bridge, and then along the left edge of a field for 200 yards to a marker post. Turn left through a gap in the trees to a stile; then right along the right edge of a field to another stile. Continue straight across a narrow lane, then along the right edge of a field, with trees to the right; here purple knapweed and other flowers in the meadow attract butterflies in summer. Enter a wood at a stile by a metal gate and keep ahead on a track with a stream-cut ravine on the right. This is ancient woodland with trees such as beech, oak, holly and birch, and carpets of bluebells in spring. Follow marker posts for the **Tunbridge Wells Circular (High Weald) Walk** footpath as it winds through trees. The path becomes narrower and descends steeply into the valley of a stream, crossing it by a plank bridge. Notice the luxuriant vegetation here, with many ferns and horsetails flourishing in the damp conditions. The path ascends the opposite bank and up steps to a marker post by a

shed at the end of a garden.

Leave the **High Weald Walk** here by going left (not diagonally right as the arrow indicates) to stay on the edge of the wood. Soon go down more steps and then ahead to cross a footbridge over a stream near a huge beech tree. Keep straight ahead on the main path through trees, finally climbing quite steeply, and soon, with fields behind the line of trees on the right, reach a stile out of the wood. Continue diagonally right across a field to a stile, taking in the views to the right. Then go diagonally left across a field with donkeys to another stile. Turn sharp right through trees, with a large pond on the right, to reach a lane.

Turn left along the lane, rather than taking the one opposite. Soon there are far-reaching views back to the right, over the hedge. Keep straight on, ignoring a lane to the right and another to the left. The lane goes downhill, bends right, and then goes gradually uphill between tall hedges, composed mostly of hazel. After following this lane for ¾ mile, a T-junction with a busier road is reached.

Go left for 100 yards; then turn left off the road at a footpath sign, to cross the drive to a somewhat unusual cottage and go through a pedestrian gate. Continue on a slightly right diagonal across a field and straight over a drive leading to the gates of

Drive and Stroll

Chilstone, to reach another pedestrian gate. Go through the gate and diagonally right across a field, aiming for the corner of a fence jutting out into the field and, beyond it, a water tower in the distance. At the corner of the fence cross a stile and walk ahead on a path between wire fences, ignoring a second stile on the left. Keep straight on where there are stiles on both sides of the path. Soon the path winds through trees, with outcrops of sandstone on both sides, to a gate and a main road. Turn left along the pavement to pass the sandstone church at **Langton Green** and reach the **Hare** pub.

The church, built in 1862 by Sir George Gilbert Scott, has stained-glass windows by the famous Pre-Raphaelite artists Edward Burne-Jones, William Morris and Charles Kempe.

To return to the recreation ground car park, turn left past the pub and follow the pavement beside the road as it passes the green and bends right; the sign for the recreation ground is soon reached on the left.

*Around the green are 16th and 17th-century cottages and **Langton House**, built in 1810 in the Regency style as the new dower house for the manor.*

Places of Interest Nearby

Penshurst Place, 3 miles to the north, dates from the 14th century and has a unique medieval baron's hall, magnificent staterooms and beautiful Tudor gardens, plus an adventure playground, shop and restaurant. Telephone: 01892 870307.

Groombridge Place Gardens, 1½ miles south-west of Langton Green, has formal walled gardens, woodland walks and an adventure trail. Telephone: 01892 863999.

3 One Tree Hill

The view from the Greensand Ridge

The Walk 3 miles
Terrain Undulating, with some uneven ground and steep climbs
Map OS Explorer 147 Sevenoaks and Tonbridge (GR 558532)

How to get there

One Tree Hill is 2 miles east of Sevenoaks and is reached by B roads going south from the A25 at Seal or north from the A21. **Parking** At GR 558532. **Public transport** Not practicable

Drive and Stroll

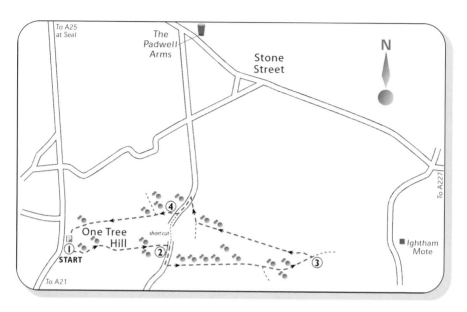

Introduction

The Greensand Ridge runs through the middle of Kent and this walk takes you along a section of it. It offers superb views over the Weald to the high ground of Ashdown Forest in the far distance. The walk is particularly glorious in spring, when there are sheets of bluebells scenting the air, and other flowers such as wood anemones, celandines and violets adding to the colourful palette. Autumn provides wonderful colours in the gold leaves of the beech and hazel and russets of oak. It is quite a strenuous walk, however, with some fairly steep ascents and descents, some on uneven ground, and sections can be muddy after wet weather. The rewards provided by the views and the flowers are well worth the effort, though, and there is also the possibility of an extension to visit the wonderful moated medieval house at Ightham Mote.

The Padwell Arms

This is a friendly pub, 1½ miles north-east of One Tree Hill. There is always a good selection of real ales and good value food such as steaks, mixed grill, seafood platter and ribs in barbecue sauce. Sandwiches and ploughman's are also available and there are children's and vegetarian meals. The interior is pleasant, with beams and old brass hunting horns and cooking pots, and there is an outdoor sitting area. Telephone: 01732 761532.

There is also a tearoom and restaurant at Ightham Mote, open when the house is open and during more limited hours in winter.

THE WALK

With your back to the road, leave the car park in the far right corner, passing an information board and go through a gap in a wooden fence. Go straight over a cross-track and ahead along an earth track. At the next cross-track, turn left. You are now on the **Greensand Way** (GW) long distance footpath and will be following its route for the next mile.

*As you walk there are fantastic views on the right over the **Low Weald** to the **High Weald** and **Ashdown Forest** in the distance. **One Tree Hill** rises to 679 ft (207m) above sea level and has a good diversity of tree species.*

Pass a huge beech tree and continue straight across a small grassy area, keeping right of a bench, and ahead on a track. Where it meets a cross-track, turn right at a marker post and then keep right at a fork; soon bend right to a stile and leave the National Trust land. The path goes steeply downhill past some large beech trunks, and there is quite a steep drop on the right, so take care, particularly if you have children with you.

This section of the walk is glorious

in spring, with the blossom of wild cherry trees and on the woodland floor a carpet of bluebells, wood anemones, celandines, primroses and violets.

When a narrow road is reached, near a house entrance, the walk goes to the right. (However, for a shorter walk, turn left onto a path that goes uphill to reach the end of a lane; follow it to where a wood starts on the left to rejoin the route at Point 4.) After going right along the lane for 100 yards, the longer walk goes left over a stile at a GW fingerpost and then soon enters the National Trust **Ightham Mote** estate.

The pink flowers of lady's smock attract orange-tip butterflies in spring, and later the pungent smell of wild garlic is evident. In spring the wood is rich in birdlife, including nuthatches, finches and warblers.

Keep straight on at a marker post. Later the path bends right down steps and turns left past a cottage. Continue gradually uphill on a track through trees and then with more views on the right. At the top of the incline you reach a stile to the right of an open gateway, with a marker post just beyond.

If you wish to visit **Ightham Mote**, go

Drive and Stroll

straight on here for ¼ mile to a lane and turn right for 50 yards to the entrance; then retrace your steps to this point. The walk continues on a broad stony track running back to the left here and uphill with open ground on the left; then into trees. As the track emerges from the trees and bends left there are views to the North Downs in the distance on the right. Keep straight ahead at a crossing of paths to go up an incline; then turn right on a cross-path in front of an orchard to reach a lane. Turn left for 300 yards.

Go right into the trees at a bridleway sign, just before the wood on the right ends. (Turn left into wood if coming from the short cut.) About 100 yards into the wood, turn left onto a cross-track, passing through mixed woodland of hazel, oak, beech and holly. Keep straight on where a path goes off right to keep on the edge of the wood with a field, then orchards, behind trees on the left. There is a narrow, muddy section downhill between tree-topped banks. Then you go uphill with a field and white house beyond to the right. Where a wooden post and rail fence starts on the left, keep ahead parallel to it; then, when it bends away left, keep straight on, going past a barrier across the path after 100 yards and ahead near the right edge of the wood. The path bends left to reach a cross-track, where you can go ahead under the fence pole at its corner and continue on a path for 150 yards to the car park. Alternatively, turn right on the cross-track for 150 yards to a lane and left for 100 yards to the car park.

Places of Interest Nearby

Ightham Mote (National Trust) is one of the finest moated manor houses in England, dating from 1330 with a great hall, Tudor chapel, gardens, woodland walks, restaurant and gift shop. Telephone: 01732 811145.

Knole House (National Trust), 2 miles to the west, is one of the largest mansions in Britain, with important collections of paintings, furniture and silver. It is set in a deer park. Telephone: 01732 450608.

4 | Hodsoll Street

Ridley Church

The Walk 3 miles
Terrain Quiet lanes and gently undulating land
Map: OS Explorer 148 Maidstone and the Medway Towns (GR 625629)

How to get there

Hodsoll Street is reached by minor roads going west from the A227 between Wrotham and Meopham. As you enter the village keep straight on (no through road) as the road bends left, to get to the village hall. **Parking** At the village hall car park. **Public transport** Not practicable

Drive and Stroll

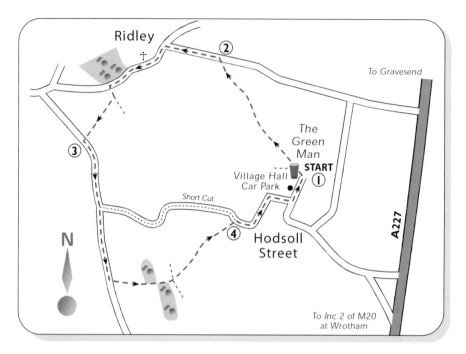

Introduction

During this walk through the undulating countryside on the top of the North Downs, with its pleasing pattern of fields and woods, you will pass an ancient church, an unusual thatched well and several old houses. Starting in the village of Hodsoll Street, with its picturesque green surrounded by attractive cottages and a pub, the route starts on field paths, where you may see some Highland cattle a long way from home. The middle section of the walk is mainly on quiet lanes, passing the old church at Ridley and the adjacent manor house. The return is across meadows, with distant views to the River Thames and Essex beyond, and then along a lane with pretty white-boarded cottages.

The Green Man

This pub at Hodsoll Street is in a lovely setting by the green. Inside the friendly, family-run pub, there are large rooms arranged around a central bar and there is also seating in the garden. The menu offers a large selection of main meals, including chicken stuffed with brie and wrapped in filo pastry, and roast duck, while tortilla wraps, filled French sticks, sandwiches and ploughman's are also available. Several cask ales are on tap. Telephone: 01732 823575.

Holywell Park

THE WALK

From the car park, continue further along the lane, soon reaching the green, which is surrounded by the pub and several attractive cottages, one built of flint with a dovecote in the garden. In front of the gates to the impressive mansion of **Holywell Park**, turn left along a tarmac track past a tile-hung cottage and a well. Where the tarmac ends, go through a wooden gate and ahead into a field. Keep alongside a metal fence on the right and when it ends go slightly diagonally right across the large field, going between two large trees and then diagonally right to the far right corner of the field; aim for the metal gates there. (You may find a small herd of Highland cattle in the field.) Go over a stile to the right of one of the gates and then continue up the next field, going slightly diagonally left to a stile about two-thirds of the way along the fence and hedge on the left boundary of the field. Maintain your previous direction across another meadow, aiming 100 yards to the right of metal barns that come into view as you walk up the slope. There are pleasant views over the rolling wooded countryside to the left before you reach a stile to a lane.

Turn left along the lane to a T-junction, then left again. You soon

23

Drive and Stroll

pass the small early Norman church at **Ridley**, built from local flint, and behind it **Ridley Court**.

Opposite the church is an unusual thatched well dating from 1810.

Continue along the lane, going downhill under trees. Soon after passing a house on the left, go left at a bridleway sign and follow a track into trees. After about 150 yards, as a fence around the garden on the left bends away left, go right through an unmarked gap in a hedge to a stile and marker post 10 yards on. Go slightly diagonally left across a field, passing 20 yards to the left of the second telegraph pole from the left of a line across the field. Notice all the flints in the chalky soil of the field, which provided a local building material in past times. At the far end of the field go through a gap in a hedge to a lane.

 ③

Go left along the lane, at first under tall holly bushes with knobbly trunks. Continue for ¼ mile until a lane goes off to the right, signed to **Fairseat** and **Wrotham**. (For a shorter walk keep straight on here to return

to **Hodsoll Street**.) For the longer loop that rejoins this lane at point 4 take the lane to the right. Soon you pass **Horns Lodge**, dating from the 15th century, on the left. Then continue gradually uphill on this lane for ⅓ mile until there are footpath signs on both sides of the road. Go left here over a stile and slightly diagonally right across a field, with views on the left to the Thames and Essex in the distance. At the end of the field keep ahead on a grassy track to the right of a small wood; then after 100 yards go left over a stile, now with a wire fence and small wood on your right. At a marker post where the fence ends, go ahead but slightly diagonally left (not sharp left) across a meadow, with isolated trees, to a stile at the far end. Continue slightly diagonally left across the next field to a stile to a lane, near an avenue of trees lining the drive to a house.

 ④

Turn right along the lane and follow it as it bends sharp left and then eventually right past white-boarded cottages. As it bends right again, take the lane going off to the left to return to the village hall.

Places of Interest Nearby

Trosley Country Park has 160 acres of downland and woodland, with a visitor centre and picnic area. It is just 2 miles south, off the A227. Telephone: 01732 823570.

5 | Ryarsh and Birling

The countryside near Birling

The Walk 3½ miles
Terrain Gently undulating on lanes and well-trodden tracks
Map OS Explorer 148 Maidstone and the Medway Towns (GR 671600)

How to get there

Ryarsh is just off the A20, 1 mile west of West Malling. From Junction 4 of the M20 go south to the A20 and then right (west) for 1 mile. Take a right turn signed to Ryarsh, turn right again at the first T-junction, then keep straight on to reach the village hall. **Parking**   At the village hall. **Public transport**   Not practicable

Drive and Stroll

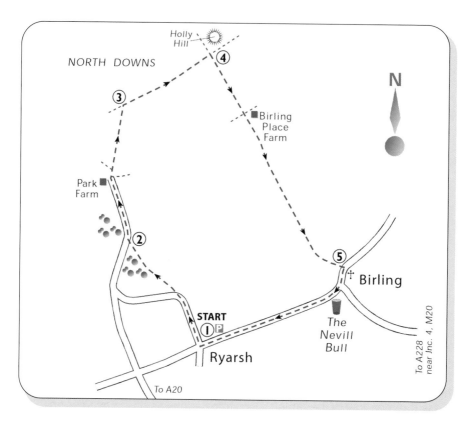

Introduction

This walk takes you up to the North Downs, with the opportunity for a picnic on the slopes. You also walk along a section of the ancient trackway used by pilgrims on their journey to Canterbury. On the hills the dark green of the yews contrasts with the pale leaves of whitebeams, and stately beeches add their fresh green foliage. Below the trees are many wild flowers in season, including violets, celandines and wild strawberries, while speckled wood butterflies dance in the dappled sunshine. There are fine views from the hills over the surrounding countryside, including the Medway valley, before you descend through fields and past an ancient manor house. You then return through Birling, with its Norman church and former blacksmith's forge, plus a welcome inn.

The Nevill Bull

This pub at Birling is named in memory of a member of the Nevill family, who owned much of the land in the area from historic times. Inside, the bar area and separate non-smoking restaurant have beams, brick walls and large fireplaces, providing pleasant surroundings for your meal. There is also an outdoor sitting area on the rear patio. The menu includes roasts, steaks, curry, seafood platter and steak and kidney pudding. There are also ploughman's, jacket potatoes and baguettes on offer and a selection of real ales. Telephone: 01732 843193.

THE WALK

Turn right out of the entrance to the car park; then, opposite the **Duke of Wellington** pub, turn right up **Chapel Lane**. Shortly after passing the chapel the lane bends left, but keep straight on here through a wide gap in the hedge and then keep left of the hedge ahead by a footpath sign. The right of way goes diagonally left across the meadow to the far left corner, but there may be a more obvious path along the right edge of the field and then going left at its end to reach a stile in the corner by a hornbeam tree. Cross the stile and keep ahead on a concrete path until it reaches a concrete road; there go left for 20 yards to a lane.

Turn right along the lane, with a damp wood on the left where you may see bright yellow marsh marigolds in spring and creamy white meadowsweet in summer. Go past **Park Farm** on the left and keep ahead to the right of a barn to continue towards the downs on a path between hedges.

On reaching a broad cross-track at the base of the hills, turn right. You are now on the ancient **Pilgrim's Way**, which is also part of the **North Downs Way** (NDW) long-distance footpath. The track goes under overhanging trees and is enclosed by trees on both sides for some distance before opening out on the right with views over the **Medway valley** and across to the **Greensand Ridge**.

There are flowers under the trees, including violets, celandines and wild strawberries in spring, and in summer the blue, nettle-leaved bellflowers. Speckled wood butterflies can be seen from April to October, their colouring of cream spots on a brown background providing good camouflage in the dappled sunshine.

Birling church

After ¼ mile, look for a gap on both sides of the track, with a marker post for the **NDW** ahead to the left. If you want a good site for a picnic, the path to the left leads up to the downland of **Holly Hill**. However, the walk continues to the right, over a stile, and then gradually downhill on the left edge of a field going away from the downs. At the base of the hedge on the left are flowers such as lilac scabious and purple knapweed and these attract butterflies such as meadow browns, gatekeepers and small tortoiseshells in summer. On reaching a concrete road, go straight across to continue downhill on a broad grassy track with a tall hedge on the left. Where the hedge ends, look back to the left to view an old house, **Birling Place Farm**. Keep ahead through a gap in a belt of trees and continue along the right edge of the next field towards **Birling church** in the distance. At the end of the field, go past a converted barn to a stile and then along the right edge of a field, with the church ahead.

The church has an impressive tower and was recorded in Domesday Book, though much of it dates from the 14th and 15th centuries.

Cross a stile and go carefully down steps to a road.

Turn right past the church and follow the road as it bends right past the site of the old forge and the **Nevill Bull pub**. Keep alongside the road as it goes through **Birling** village and between fields to reach **Ryarsh** and the car park.

Places of Interest Nearby

The Museum of Kent Life, 6 miles east of Ryarsh, is an open-air museum with old buildings, demonstration gardens and orchards, tearoom and shop. Telephone: 01622 763936.

6 Wateringbury

The mill pond at Wateringbury

The Walk 3¼ or 6 miles
Terrain Hilly, though there is a shortcut that avoids the steepest climb.
Map OS Explorer 148 Maidstone & the Medway Towns (GR 692534)

How to get there

From the crossroads on the A26 in the centre of Wateringbury, turn south on the B2015. **Parking** Following the turn, there is a car park almost immediately on the right. **Public transport** Wateringbury railway station is on the route.

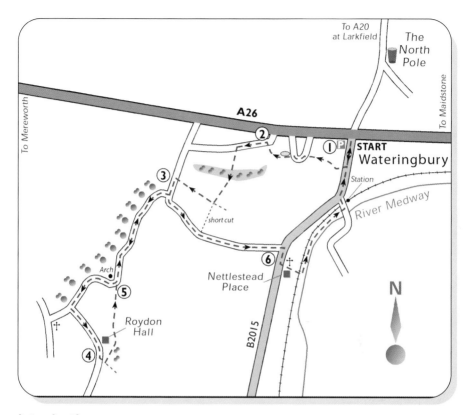

Introduction

This moderately strenuous walk takes you to the hidden part of Wateringbury, past orchards to the attractive group of buildings near the millpond, now used only by ducks and coots. After another section through orchards, flushed with blossom in spring, the walk goes through the edge of the strangely-named hamlet of Pizien Well. There follows a steep climb on a lane up the side of the valley and past a fine archway in the grounds of Mereworth Castle. The 16th-century mansion of Roydon Hall is also passed and there is the opportunity for a short diversion to view the exterior of a disused medieval church. You then descend into the valley, with superb views over the Medway valley to the high ground in the distance. The final section passes the 15th-century church and medieval manor at Nettlestead before returning alongside the River Medway, where there are swans and many pleasure boats on the water.

Drive and Stroll

The North Pole

This friendly pub is 1 mile north of the crossroads on the A26 at Wateringbury, on the road to Larkfield. It has a bar, separate eating area and a large garden. Meals include Lancashire hot-pot and smoked haddock pasta with prawns and mushrooms, and there are also salads, baguettes, ploughman's, jacket potatoes and sandwiches. The unusual name of the pub probably refers to one of the main support poles in a hop garden. Telephone: 01622 812392.

The **Riverside Restaurant**, passed on the walk, often serves lunches and teas in the summer.

THE WALK

Turn right out of the entrance to the car park and walk downhill alongside the road, passing the village lock-up, built in 1842. Then, 50 yards after **Warden Mill Close**, turn right on a rough track (no footpath sign at time of writing). The track goes past houses and then bends right between hedges, with orchards to the right. On reaching a lane in front of a white-boarded converted oast house turn left. As the lane bends right past a former mill house, keep straight on to the left of a lovely duck pond, which once supplied water for the mill. Keep straight ahead after 100 yards as a tarmac track bends off left, to continue on a wide path between the trees lining the pond and a hedge. You pass some large horse chestnut trees and walk beside the stream that feeds the pond before going between houses to a lane.

Turn left along the lane and, 150 yards after passing Manor Farm with its white-cowled oasts, turn left at a footpath sign to walk on a stony track between fields. Cross a footbridge over a stream; then keep ahead on a wide track through a small wood, with ferns and giant horsetails. After emerging from the trees, keep straight on to the left of a metal gate and then along the left edge of a field, with a tall hedge on the left and soon with orchards on the right. After about 350 yards up a gradual slope, you reach a cross-track, which to the left is lined with tall poplars. (For a shorter walk, avoiding a fairly steep climb, keep straight on here to reach a lane after a few hundred yards. Then turn left to reach a main road; from there you follow instructions from point 6.) The longer walk continues to the right on the cross-track, which is grassy and goes between orchards, with views over the valley to the right. Later there are trees on the right – first a line of cut-down poplars and then sweet chestnuts – before the path goes between hedges to a lane by houses.

Go left along the lane; then after

The Triumphal Arch at Mereworth Castle

300 yards turn right into another lane. This lane soon bends left and climbs increasingly steeply under overhanging trees.

*On the right is a wood with some magnificent beech and sweet chestnut trees, and carpets of wood anemones and celandines in spring. As the lane bends right, there is something of a surprise in the form of a large ornate sandstone arch on the right. This marks the boundary of the grounds of the **Mereworth Castle** estate. **Mereworth Castle**, unfortunately not visible from the road and not open to the public, isn't a castle but an 18th-century mansion, built in the Palladian style.*

The lane goes downhill for a while, with good views to the left, and then uphill again. Turn left along **Roydon Hall Road**, unless you want to view the exterior of the disused 15th-century **East Peckham church**, which is 400 yards further uphill on the lane, before returning to this point. After turning left, the road takes you past the entrance to **Roydon Hall**, and then continues past the ancient manor house, built in 1535 and now home to a transcendental meditation movement.

About 300 yards past the house, go left at a wooden fingerpost and up a bank into trees. As you emerge from the trees after 150 yards, go sharp left on a path alongside more trees, soon with a view of the manor and its

Drive and Stroll

gardens, including a large cedar. Cross a stile and follow the path through trees, with a wall to the left. On leaving the trees, follow a grassy path round to the left for 250 yards to a short marker post; then go slightly diagonally right for 100 yards to another. From here, go ahead on a stony track that soon becomes a grassy track, aiming for the arch that you passed earlier and keeping about 200 yards left of a communications mast. There are superb views on the left to the disused church and back to the **High Weald** in the distance. Opposite the arch, go through a gap to the left of a metal gate and onto a lane.

Turn right to retrace part of the outward journey, but now going downhill with magnificent views over the **Medway Valley** to the **North Downs** in the distance. When the lane reaches a T-junction with another, turn right and follow it round a left bend; on the right is a small wood with the pink flowers of red campion and herb Robert on the bank. Continue on the lane as it runs between apple and pear orchards, reaching a main road after ¾ mile.

Go right alongside the road for 200 yards and cross with care to go through a lychgate and onto a path to the church at **Nettlestead**.

In 1763, during a terrible storm, all the windows of the church were broken by hailstones, some of which were 10 inches across.

By the church porch, follow a path to the right and then go along the right edge of the churchyard to leave it through a stone arch. On the right are the grounds of **Nettlestead Place**, a medieval manor. Continue down a damp field to carefully cross a railway via stiles and reach the bank of the **River Medway**. Turn left on the path, passing trees and then the pleasure boats moored on both sides of the river. Often you will also see swans and Canada geese on the water here. Just after passing **Riverside Cottage and Restaurant**, bear left up to a busy road and turn left over the railway crossing near an old signal box. Turn right alongside a busier road, following the bend and passing the station entrance. Continue gradually uphill for ⅓ mile to reach the car park.

Places of Interest Nearby

The Hop Farm Country Park, 6 miles south-west of Wateringbury, has shire horses, farm and pet animals, an adventure playground, exhibitions, a gift shop and a restaurant. Telephone: 01622 872068.

Yalding Organic Gardens, 3 miles south of Wateringbury, have a series of demonstration gardens of different periods, all cultivated organically. There is a café, and plants are on sale. Telephone: 01622 814650.

7 Otham

The North Downs from Otham

The Walk 3¾ miles
Terrain Gently undulating, apart from one short but steep climb
Map OS Explorer 148 Maidstone and the Medway Towns (GR 789543)

How to get there

From the A20, 2 miles east of Maidstone, turn south at Willington Street and after ½ mile turn left into Deringwood Drive. **Parking** After ¼ mile there are car parks behind the shops and Downswood Community Centre on the left. **Public transport** There are buses to Downswood from Maidstone.

Drive and Stroll

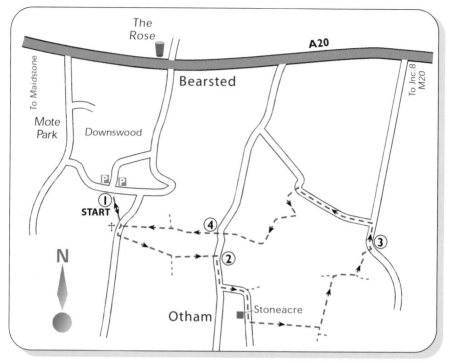

Introduction

Although this walk starts on the outskirts of Maidstone, it has some lovely surprises in the form of beautiful scenery and wonderful medieval timbered houses. There is no longer any evidence of the ragstone quarry that provided stone for the City and Tower of London, but instead there are gentle green valleys, grazed by sheep, and views across the valley of the River Len to the North Downs. You pass a 12th-century church, orchards of apples and pears, and plantations of strawberries and raspberries.

The Rose Inn

This pub is on the A20 in Bearsted, 1 mile north of the start of the walk. It has been refurbished and provides pleasant surroundings for your meal. There is a good choice of food, including sea bass stuffed with lemon, dill and parsley, and poached chicken breast topped with Stilton and chive cream, as well as lighter meals such as moules marinières, salads and baguettes. There is also a selection of beers and wines. Telephone: 01622 738200.

THE WALK

Turn right in front of the row of shops on **Deringwood Drive** and, where they end, cross the road and go along a tarmac path opposite. The path goes gradually uphill between hedges, with houses beyond, to reach a lane. Go straight ahead for 100 yards, then opposite the lychgate of Otham church go through a gap in a hedge at a footpath sign and slightly diagonally right across a large field.

Otham church dates back to Norman times and has an impressive crownpost roof in the nave. The churchyard has a memorial to William Stevens, an 18th-century author whose pen-name was 'Nobody', paid for by the Society of Nobody's Friends.

As you walk there are views to the North Downs on the left and back over Maidstone and the Medway valley. Just over halfway across the field, the path divides at a fingerpost: take the left fork to go ahead towards houses and then past a metal gate and a converted barn to a lane.

Turn right to go past **Madam Taylor's**, a medieval manor house. Then, just past the war memorial and the village sign (illustrating the tools used by village craftsmen over the ages), turn left along a narrow lane. The lane goes steeply downhill, skirting ponds, and then bends right uphill to pass the National Trust property of **Stoneacre**, a half-timbered yeoman's house dating from the late 15th century, and its lovely garden. About 150 yards past the entrance, look for a short marker post by the fence on the right and turn left on a rough road between a barn and a house. When the track ends (100 yards), keep ahead over a stile to the left of a gate and continue straight on, crossing two more stiles next to gates. Keep ahead on a grassy track, now with a fence on the right. Then, past a telegraph pole, go ahead on a track to the right of a cane fruit plantation. Where the hedge on the right ends, go through a gap ahead to a broad cross-track with tall poplars beyond. Turn left on the track, now with a tall hedge on the left, and orchards on the right. As the orchards end, go diagonally right for 100 yards to reach a line of tall poplars and turn right alongside them. Where they end turn left towards the downs, now with poplars on the right. Follow the track as it bends left and right to skirt a garden and reach a lane.

It is worth going 100 yards to the right here to see a lovely black and white timbered house called **'Cordwainers'**, but the walk continues to the left along the lane for 300 yards then goes left along

Drive and Stroll

Caring Road. This lane goes gradually downhill between tall hedges, passes a large fishing lake and then climbs past Caring House with its impressive door. The lane bends left and right past the entrance to Jacksons; then, 500 yards on, as it bends sharp right, go left at the fingerpost for the **Len Valley Walk**. From the gateway go left almost immediately through a gap in a line of poplars and then turn right to walk alongside them. Where they end, don't go through the gap ahead, but instead bear left past a short marker post and along the right edge of a meadow, with a bank on the right and oasts ahead to the left. Keep ahead for 80 yards as the bank ends; then turn right at a marker post to go through a gap in a hedge. Go diagonally right across a field, aiming for the right end of a hedge line at the far end, to reach a stile and marker post rather hidden at the corner of the hedge. Cross the stile and turn sharp right along the right edge of a field to another stile; then bear left along a long field, going across the slope and keeping left of all but the last three of the tall trees in a line along the middle of the field. Go over a stile in the far corner of the field and then steeply up the left edge of a field towards farm buildings. Continue through a kissing gate and ahead for 100 yards to a track that goes between farm buildings, then houses, to a lane.

Go straight across to a concrete footpath sign and ahead on a path between hedges and then with a field on the left and a tall hedge on the right, and with **Otham church** soon visible ahead. Continue on the right edge of the field to reach a lane near the church; then cross to the right to go past bollards and onto the tarmac path leading back to the car park.

Places of Interest Nearby

Stoneacre (National Trust), passed on the walk, has limited opening times. Telephone 01622 862871.

Leeds Castle, just east of Otham, is a lovely moated castle with gardens, aviary, maze, restaurant and shops. Telephone: 01622 765400.

8 | Bewl Water

The man-made lake known as Bewl Water

The Walk 3¾ miles
Terrain Gently undulating, apart from one short but steep climb
Map OS Explorer 148 Maidstone and the Medway Towns (GR 789543)

How to get there

Bewl Water is reached by an access road from the A21, 1 mile south of
Lamberhurst. **Parking** At the reservoir; there is a charge for car parking.
Public transport Not practicable

Drive and Stroll

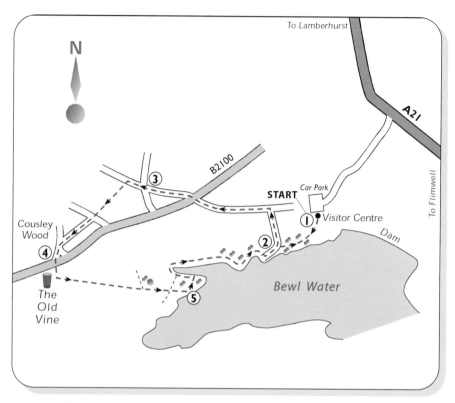

Introduction

The highlights of this walk are the lovely views over the man-made lake at Bewl Water, a huge reservoir formed by damming the stream along a valley, and now used for sailing, angling and other aquatic activities. The walk goes through woods that are carpeted with bluebells in spring and then makes an inland loop using quiet lanes, with views over the reservoir. You pass a fine inn in the village of Cousley Wood before returning to Bewl Water along a tarmac track with banks colourful with wild flowers. After going through woodland, the final section is along the bank of the reservoir; here birds such as great crested grebes share the water with yachts and fishermen. At the visitor centre there is a café, gift shop and adventure playground, and boat trips are available.

The Old Vine

This pub at Cousley Wood is passed on the walk. It is an attractive old coaching inn with low-beamed ceilings, timbered floor and open log fire in an inglenook fireplace. You can eat in the bar area or in a separate, more formal restaurant. The menu includes fillet steak in a port and mushroom sauce and beer-battered cod and chips, plus a large selection of specials, basket meals and sandwiches. Telephone: 01892 782271.

There is also a self-service restaurant at Bewl Water, offering meals and snacks.

THE WALK

From the car park go down to the side of the visitor centre that faces the lake and turn right past the windows of the café and its outdoor sitting area to go on a gravel path into trees. Keep right at a sign pointing left to the adventure playground and go straight across a narrow road into more trees (signed **Round Bewl Walk**). On reaching a road with lots of boats parked behind, turn left for 30 yards; then turn right in front of the **Rowing Club** to go past the boats. After 100 yards, go diagonally left at a fingerpost, into trees and down steps. You soon go up more steps and reach a minor road near a house.

Turn right up the road and at a T-junction turn left. Take care walking along the narrow road, which has tall banks where the sandstone rock is exposed; here mosses and ferns grow luxuriantly in the damp, shady conditions. At a gap by a gate on the left there is a view back over the reservoir, but the walk continues along the road past **Ladymeads Farm** with its oast house. At a crossroads go straight across with care and along **Sleepers Stile Road**, with its tall hedges of holly, hazel and other shrubs.

At the next crossroads, by a small, triangular green, keep straight ahead. After 300 yards, as telegraph wires cross the road, turn left on a track under overhanging trees. This track, which can be muddy in places, has lovely yellow celandines alongside in spring, under the fresh green foliage of beech trees. On reaching a road, go straight across and along the lane opposite. As you walk there are distant views to Bewl Water over the hedge on the left and later there is a field where you may see some Jacob's sheep. At the T-junction, turn left; then, after 60 yards, keep right at a fork to reach the main road, with the **Old Vine** pub at **Cousley Wood** opposite on the right.

Bewl Water seen from the walk

④

Cross the road carefully and go down the narrow private road opposite. Continue on the road as it bends left, soon with a fine view of the reservoir in the valley on the left. In spring the banks of the road are colourful with wild flowers, including bluebells, pink lady's smock, yellow archangel and white stitchwort, and you may see orange tip, peacock and small tortoiseshell butterflies. At a marker post on the right, opposite a 'slow, children' sign on the left, continue straight ahead along the road. Where the road swings right by **Bewl Water Oast**, turn left through a kissing gate to walk alongside its garden.

Oast houses were used to dry the hops used in making beer, and the number of them in this part of Kent illustrates its former importance as a hop-growing area.

Keep straight on at a marker post by a barn to continue between fences, with a bluebell wood on the left. The path bends left and right; then the fence on the right ends at a broad cross-track.

 ⑤

Turn left on the track to reach the edge of the reservoir and at the water's edge turn left again to go round an inlet and continue on the obvious path, keeping aware of the cyclists who share it. There are often great crested grebes on the water here. After passing more trees, with bluebells and wood anemones beneath in spring, you reach a fence where you turn left past a gate to follow a narrow road uphill. Where the road bends left by a house turn right through a gap in the fence to go down steps. You are now retracing the outward journey through trees and the boatyard to get back to the visitor centre.

Bewl Water is the largest lake in the south-east and provides water for a large population.

Places of Interest Nearby

Scotney Castle Garden (National Trust) is 1 mile north of Bewl. The superb garden surrounds the picturesque remains of a moated 14th-century castle. Telephone: 01892 891081.

9 | Hawkhurst

The path near Hawkhurst

The Walk 2 miles
Terrain Gently undulating on lanes and field paths
Map OS Explorer 136 The Weald (GR 764305)

How to get there

Hawkhurst is at the junction of the A229 and the A268. **Parking** There is a car park north of the A268 at the eastern end of the village. **Public transport** Buses from Maidstone and Tunbridge Wells use the bus station near the car park.

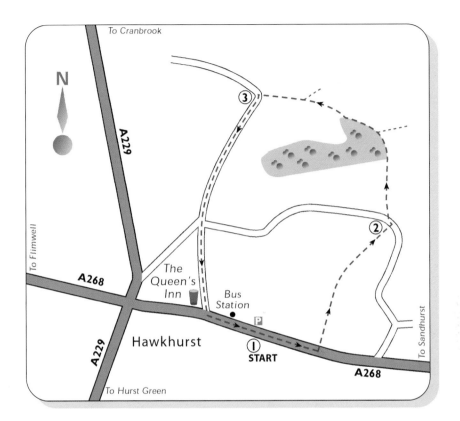

Introduction

This walk near the border of Kent and Sussex includes a fine view to the neighbouring county and takes you through the lovely undulating countryside that is a feature of this area. You walk through buttercup meadows and on field paths, then through woodland full of wild garlic, before returning to Hawkhurst along a quiet lane with wild flowers colouring the hedgebanks.

Back in the village there is a selection of inns and shops, including some along an unusual weatherboarded colonnade, and a café. The Hawkhurst Gang was a group of smugglers which terrorized the area between 1735 and 1749, bringing in contraband goods from the south coast and using many of the local inns. More recently, Hawkhurst acquired a place in the history of the English car industry, as William Rootes had a cycle shop here before setting up the company that made Hillman, Humber and Sunbeam cars.

Drive and Stroll

The Queen's Inn

This was first recorded as an inn in the 16th century and is a handsome, wisteria-covered building with a Georgian façade. At one time during its long history, it is said to have been a haunt of the notorious Hawkhurst Gang. Inside there is comfortable seating in the wine bar and restaurant, which has ancient oak beams, tapestries and a big inglenook fireplace. From a wide choice of meals, examples include Norfolk duck breast in a cherry kirsch jus, and salmon and prosciutto. There are also children's and vegetarian meals, baguettes, salads and ploughman's. Outside, there is a garden and courtyard. Telephone: 01580 753577.

THE WALK

Go out from the car park entrance and turn left on the path alongside the main road for ¼ mile. As you pass the village sign, there is a fine view to the right over into Sussex. Continue past the lodge of **Fowlers Park House** (the rhododendrons in the grounds are colourful in late spring); then, opposite **Hawkhurst Place**, a fine black and white timbered building, go left through a pedestrian gate at a footpath sign. Go under holly bushes and alongside a fence to a stile and then straight on past a large ash tree on the left, soon with an excellent view ahead over the undulating Wealden countryside. Keep near to the left edge of the field to reach a gateway in a fence; then go diagonally right across the next field, a lovely buttercup meadow, aiming just to the left of a red-tiled roof ahead. At the end of the meadow you reach a stile, 5 yards to the left of a gateway, with an attractive white-boarded house and converted barn to the right.

Cross the stile to a lane and turn left for a few yards; then go right at a

---

Places of Interest Nearby

The National Pinetum, Bedgebury, lies 4 miles north-west of Hawkhurst. It has over 200 species of tree, set in a beautiful landscape around lakes, plus a visitor centre. Telephone: 01580 211044.

Bodiam Castle (National Trust) is situated 4 miles to the south. It is a superb moated castle dating from the 14th century. There is a shop and tearoom. Telephone: 01580 830436.

Hawkhurst Place

footpath sign and along the left edge of a field to a metal gate. Make sure you close it behind you and then proceed along the left edge of the next field, with a line of oak trees and then a wood on your left. At the bottom of the field, as the field boundary curves right, continue beside the wood for 50 yards and then enter it at a stile. Continue ahead through the wood, with a wide stream in a deep gully to your right, and the pungent smell of wild garlic in the air. As the wood ends, keep ahead to the right of a water treatment works; then the path becomes a road, which soon passes mobile homes to reach a T-junction.

Turn left to go gradually uphill along the lane, with wild flowers such as white stitchwort and hedge parsley, blue germander speedwell and pink herb Robert colouring the banks. At a crossroads keep straight ahead along **Queen's Road** to reach the main road, with the Queen's Inn on the right; turn left to return to the car park or bus station.

10 Benenden

The remains of a windmill seen on the walk

The Walk 4½ miles
Terrain Quiet lanes and well-defined paths through gently rolling countryside; one stretch prone to mud in wet weather
Map OS Explorer 125 Romney Marsh (GR 811328)

How to get there

Benenden is on the B2086 between Cranbrook and Rolvenden. **Parking** At the car park by the village hall, south of the road. **Public transport** There are buses from Tenterden and Tunbridge Wells.

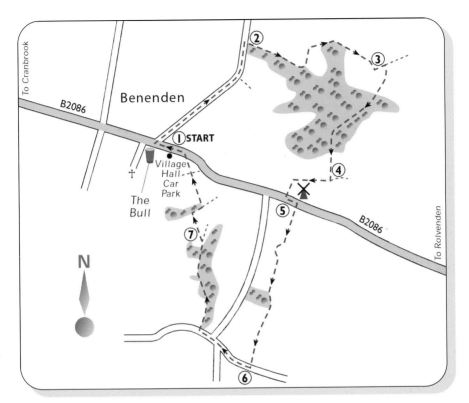

Introduction

This walk is in the heart of the Kentish Weald and uses quiet lanes and field paths to take you through the lovely rolling countryside. You walk through woods and past orchards that are fragrant with blossom in spring and colourful with fruit in late summer. The walk passes the remains of a windmill and provides superb views over miles of countryside as you return through sheep-grazed fields to Benenden. The village has a choice of hostelries, as well as a lovely church, an old schoolhouse and attractive cottages around a picturesque green.

The Bull

This pub at Benenden dates from the 17th century, a history reflected in its beams and huge inglenook fireplace. It has a spacious bar area in addition to a non-smoking restaurant and a courtyard garden. The varied menu includes swordfish steak and Mediterranean ratatouille or walnut and Stilton

Drive and Stroll

quiche. There are also toasted ciabatta sandwiches, ploughman's, and a children's menu. Telephone: 01580 240054.

THE WALK

Walking out of the car park, turn left for 50 yards; then cross the road to go past the war memorial and up **Walkhurst Road**. After passing a converted oast house, there is a view to the left over fields to **Benenden School** at the left end of a distant ridge.

The school occupies a mock-Elizabethan house, built in the 19th century by Lord Cranbrook to replace an original house of that period; he also rebuilt most of the village. One of Benenden's most famous pupils is the Princess Royal.

Ignore a stile on the right as the lane bends left and continue downhill on the lane, with flowers such as hemp agrimony and great willowherb alongside in summer. About 100 yards after the lane enters a wood and just after it crosses a deeply cut stream, go right at a wooden fingerpost just before the drive to a house.

Walk through trees, parallel to the stream, on a path that can be muddy after wet weather. (In July and August you may see broad-

The old schoolhouse at Benenden

leaved helleborine, a type of orchid, here. On the debit side, you may also encounter hungry mosquitoes!) Just before the trees end look for a yellow marker arrow on a tree trunk and follow the main track as it bends left. After 300 yards, take the right fork in the path, soon with orchards behind the trees on the left and ponds beneath trees to the right. As the wood ends, continue on a wide grassy track between hedges.

③

After a few hundred yards the track bends right and then bends left, with a wooden gate on the right. Continue on the track; then, 50 yards past the second bend, look for a stile hidden in the hedge on the right. Cross it and go diagonally right across a field to enter a wood at a stile in the far right corner. Go over a footbridge and then diagonally right for 70 yards and left up a bank at a marker arrow on a tree. Turn right at the top of the bank to go through a gap in a wire fence and ahead on a track through conifer trees. Keep on the track as it becomes wider and later bends slightly left. Continue uphill, with an orchard behind trees on the right, a plantation of young conifers on the left, and beyond it a view to the North Downs in the distance.

④

Where the orchard and conifer plantation end, go straight across a cross-track and through a gap in a hedge; then turn immediately right along the grassy verge of a field, with a tall hedge on your right. In the distance ahead is the tower of a disused windmill and a phone mast to its left. At a marker post, go right through a gap in the hedge and immediately left on a track alongside an orchard. After 100 yards, as the track goes downhill, turn left over a double stile hidden in the hedge and then go straight across a field. The windmill tower comes into close focus on the left and there are good views to the right, before you reach a stile to a road.

⑤

Take great care as you turn left along the busy road for 100 yards before turning right at a footpath sign to go through a gap in the hedge and along the left edge of a field. Continue through a gap in a tall hedge; then go slightly diagonally right across the next field to go through another gap in a hedge by a telegraph pole with marker arrows. Skirt right of the farm buildings and continue on a stony track past a converted barn. As the track bends right, go left on a grassy track for 30 yards and through a gap; then turn right to walk on the right edge of a field next to the hedge, with splendid vistas ahead to distant hills. Continue through a gateway and along the right edge of the next field to a stile by a metal gate. Keep straight on to

Drive and Stroll

the left of a fallen tree and through a line of trees, now with a tremendous view ahead, including a windmill in the distance. Go down the field under telegraph wires; then, after a large oak tree, veer left, away from the wires, to a stile to the left of a gate and onto a lane.

Turn right along the lane, keeping straight on where another joins from the left and then taking the left fork 150 yards further on. This lane is marked as part of the High Weald Landscape Trail, a long-distance footpath, which you now follow back to **Benenden**. As the lane goes into trees, turn right at a marker post to go up a bank to a stile and then sharp right up the right edge of a field to a stile in the far right corner and enter a wood. After leaving the wood over a stile, continue on the right edge of a field beside trees;

then, as the field edge bends left, keep straight ahead under overhanging trees (no marker) to a stile set back in trees. Walk through the wood on a wide track to a stile.

From the stile don't go straight across the field to an obvious stile but instead head diagonally left up the field, aiming for the left end of the fence and hedge at the far side. Cross a stile to a wide stony track and turn right for 100 yards, with a fine view to the right; then go left over a stile next to gates. Go through a narrow belt of trees and directly across a field for 100 yards to a stile; go diagonally left up the next field to another stile. Head diagonally right over the next field to a stile in the far corner by a gate to the road; here turn left for 200 yards to reach the car park.

Places of Interest Nearby

Sissinghurst Castle Garden (National Trust), 3 miles north of Benenden, is a world famous connoisseur's garden in the grounds of the remains of an Elizabethan mansion. Telephone: 01580 710700.

11 Headcorn

Near Headcorn

The Walk 2¾ miles
Terrain Mainly level on lanes and field paths
Map OS Explorer 137 Ashford (GR 835442)

How to get there

Headcorn is on the A274 between Maidstone and Tenterden. **Parking** Travelling from Maidstone the car park is on the right-hand side of the main street, next to Sainsbury's. **Public transport** Headcorn has a mainline railway station, also off the main street.

Drive and Stroll

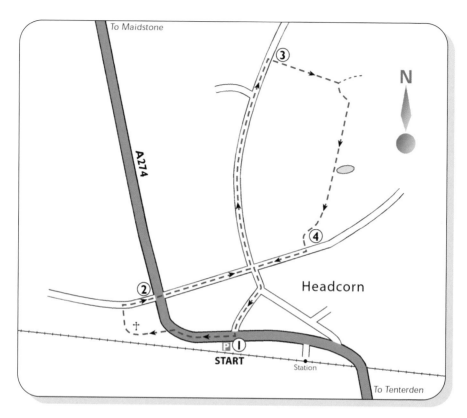

Introduction

Headcorn and the surrounding area contain a wealth of buildings of historical interest, and this walk provides the opportunity to see some of them. The route passes several medieval hall-houses with timber frames, an ancient church, and the site of a tree under which King John is reputed to have sat. Quiet lanes take you past more old houses.The return journey is along field paths leading past ponds and streams back to the village. Here you will find a selection of teashops and pubs to provide refreshment, and a variety of interesting shops.

The Village Tea Rooms

These tearooms, on the main street in Headcorn, have some comfortable sitting areas and a gift shop to tempt you. The food is also enticing, with lovely cakes, cream teas and also light meals such as pizza, quiches, soup, salads and omelettes, in addition to sandwiches and baguettes. Telephone: 01622 890682.

THE WALK

Go out of the entrance to the car park (or station) and turn left down the main street. Pass some lovely timbered houses and, as the road bends right, continue through the lychgate into the churchyard.

The size of the church reflects the wealth of the village in medieval times, thanks to the cloth trade. The outstanding feature is the 14th-century wooden roof. Near the church until recently stood an enormous oak tree with a girth of 42 feet, under which King John was reputed to have sat while watching bear-baiting.

Keep on the path that goes to the left of the church, past its porch, and then bends right to a gap in the corner of the churchyard. Ahead is **Headcorn Manor**, a very attractive black and white timbered house with lovely oriel windows. Continue ahead along **Gooseneck Lane**, now no more than a tarmac path. On reaching a road, turn right and continue alongside it to get back to the main road.

Cross with care to go along **Kings Road** opposite, passing a school and a green with large oak trees; then, after 300 yards, turn left along **Ulcombe Road**. After passing houses, the road crosses a stream and becomes narrower as it passes a recreation ground and allotments. Continue along the lane for almost ¾ mile. (In autumn the hedges are red with hawthorn berries and rosehips.) You pass a superb timbered house with a pond and oasts. Take care as you walk around a bend past a narrow lane going off to the left. Soon there is another black and white timbered house on the right.

At the end of its garden, turn right through a wide gap by a footpath sign hidden behind the hedge, to walk along the right edge of a long field. To the left are views to the Greensand Ridge in the distance. At the end of the field, cross a footbridge and then go diagonally right across a large field, initially aiming for the middle telegraph pole of three in the field. Maintain direction as you pass just to the

Places of Interest Nearby

Biddenden Vineyards, 4 miles south-east of Headcorn, has guided tours of the vineyards in addition to tastings of the wines and ciders produced there. Telephone: 01580 291726.

One of the many timbered houses in Headcorn

right of the pole and continue to the far corner of the field where the path goes over a stream; on the left is a pond that is fringed by trees and full of reed mace (often called bulrushes). From here, go ahead across the next field, keeping 20 yards to the right of a hedge jutting out into the field 80 yards ahead on the left. Aim for a gap in a line of trees at the far end of the field, about 200 yards left of the cowls of oast houses in the distance. Go through the gap, with a pond on the right, and then go diagonally right across a smaller meadow to a stile by a metal gate to a road.

Turn right for 300 yards; then go left down **Forge Lane** (signed to Smarden and Bethersden) and continue beside the road as it bends right past the end of **Oak Lane**. Finally, the road passes some attractive cottages, including the former forge, before reaching the main street in **Headcorn**, with the car park opposite to the right and the railway station to the left.

12 Rodmersham

Looking across to Rodmersham church

The Walk 3½ miles
Terrain Gently undulating on lanes and tracks
Map OS Explorer 149 Sittingbourne and Faversham (GR 916613)

How to get there

Rodmersham Green is reached by minor roads going south from the A2 at Sittingbourne or Bapchild. **Parking** Beside the village green; please park with consideration. **Public transport** Not practicable.

Drive and Stroll

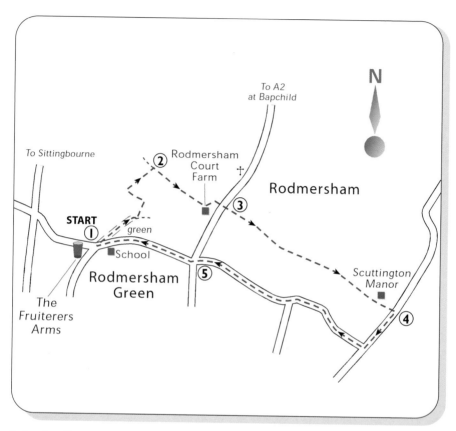

Introduction

This walk on the North Downs south of Sittingbourne has superb views over the Swale estuary to the Isle of Sheppey. Starting at the attractive village of Rodmersham Green, where pretty cottages line the green, you follow field paths and tracks past sheep-grazed meadows and orchards of apples, pears and cherries, bright with blossom in spring. After passing the ancient church at Rodmersham, the return is along lanes lined with hedges of blackthorn, hazel and alder and past a medieval house to the village green and adjacent inn.

The Fruiterers Arms

This pub at Rodmersham Green was built in 1789, originally as a farm dwelling with five acres of orchards, and was owned by Jesse Thomas, a fruiterer: hence the choice of name made when it was registered as an inn in the middle of the 19th century. Today it has a very comfortable and nicely furnished restaurant in addition to a bar area and garden. A wide range of food is served, plus local Shepherd Neame ales. Main meals include pork fillet in apple and cider sauce, and cajun and rib combo, while there are also lighter meals such as ham, egg and chips, basket and vegetarian meals, omelettes and burgers, plus sandwiches and ploughman's. Telephone: 01795 424198.

THE WALK

As you go away from the pub, walk on the narrow road along the left side of the village green, passing some picturesque cottages. Where the road ends, keep ahead to the right to go over a stile between a wooden gate and the brick-built **Providence Chapel**, dating from 1848 but now converted to a dwelling. Go straight on along the left edge of a field, with far-reaching views ahead to the Swale estuary and the Isle of Sheppey beyond it. After 100 yards, follow the field edge as it bends left alongside a fence to a stile. Keep straight on for another 200 yards and then turn right on a grassy track in front of a windbreak of poplars. Walk alongside the poplars, noticing the yellow and grey lichens growing on the bark. Then, where they end, go over a stile next to a metal gate to reach a narrow tarmac road.

Turn right on the road and follow it past pear orchards on the left and, later, younger orchards behind an alder windbreak on the right. Rodmersham's **13th-century church** comes into sight ahead on the left, with cherry orchards providing a foreground of white blossom in spring. As you reach some buildings there are old mulberry trees supported by props. Keep straight ahead on the road between farm buildings, then bend left and right to reach a lane.

Just to the right here is **Rodmersham House**, an early 17th-century manor house behind an early 19th-century east front, but the walk continues by crossing the road slightly to the right, to go through a kissing gate to the left of a white gate. Continue ahead on a track; then, where it ends, go slightly diagonally right across a field to a stile about halfway along the hedge at the far end. As you cross the field there are more magnificent views to the Swale estuary on the left. Cross the stile and go straight ahead over a sheep-grazed meadow, aiming for the left corner of a small wood, where you go through a metal gate and ahead on a rough track. The wood,

Drive and Stroll

comprising mainly sweet chestnut, is now on your right. Continue on the road past a house and then **Scuttington Manor**, to reach a lane.

④

Turn right along the lane for 500 yards, then take the next right turn, into another lane.

On the right is a blackthorn hedge, covered with starry white flowers in spring, and further along the lane there is hazel, providing colourful catkins in late winter. The ivy that clambers over the hedge flowers in autumn and attracts many insects, including red admiral and comma butterflies, to feed on the nectar and so boost their energy reserves for the winter. You pass a group of buildings which includes **New Orchard Farm**. *Orchard Farm dates from the 16th century and was once owned by the dean and chapter of Rochester Cathedral.*

Soon the lane bends left to a T-junction, where you turn right along **Upper Rodmersham Road**.

The lane is lined by tall alders on the right, recognized by their distinctive seed cones, which are often visited by birds such as siskins and linnets, and later there is field maple, with golden-yellow leaves in autumn.

The lane goes downhill under trees and then up to a T-junction.

⑤

Go left for 20 yards and then take the right fork to follow the road back to **Rodmersham Green**, taking great care, as this stretch of road can be quite busy and there are some bends with reduced visibility. You pass **Bakers Cottages**, an attractive building dating back to the 15th century, and then reach the green.

Places of Interest Nearby

Sittingbourne and Kemsley Light Railway runs steam-hauled passenger trains on a 4-mile return journey from Sittingbourne to Kemsley Down. There is a souvenir shop, and refreshments are available. Telephone: 01622 755313.

Oad Street Centre, 4 miles west of Rodmersham, has an art gallery, gift shop and restaurant. Telephone: 01795 843130.

13 | Faversham

Restored sailing barges on Faversham creek

The Walk 4¾ miles
Terrain Generally level and even
Map OS Explorer 149 Sittingbourne and Faversham (GR 015615)

How to get there

Faversham is easily reached from junction 6 of the M2.
Parking There are several car parks in the town, but the most convenient for the start of the walk is the pay and display car park off North Lane.
Public transport Faversham railway station is ½ mile from the start of the walk.

Drive and Stroll

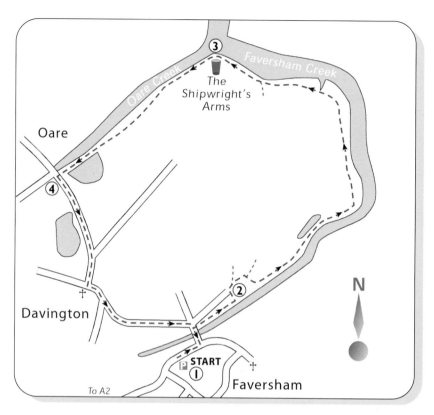

Introduction

The historic town of Faversham with its wealth of medieval houses makes a fine setting for the start of this walk. The route takes you along the bank of Faversham Creek, a stretch of water which led to the town's importance in the past as a port. You may see restored sailing barges as well as many modern yachts and some old warehouses. It is worth taking binoculars, as the creek and its banks are rich in birdlife. Past an inn with interesting maritime relics, there are more boats alongside Oare Creek before the return through the outskirts of Faversham, passing an ancient church, once part of a priory, and the site of former gunpowder works.

Do leave time to explore the town and sample the locally-brewed beer. Faversham has a fine selection of historic buildings with many from the 16th and 17th centuries surviving in Abbey Street, while in the market place is the guildhall, supported on an open arcade. The original hall was built in 1574, but this is a replacement of 1819.

The Shipwright's Arms

This old pub, situated at the junction of Faversham and Oare creeks, is passed on the walk. It is an atmospheric place, full of nautical memorabilia such as pictures and models of boats arranged around the beamed alcoves. The building dates back to the 17th century, and the large brick fireplace helps to create a cosy scene. True to its position on the edge of the water, the menu includes local sea bass and sole, and there are also smoked haddock and spring onion fish cakes and chicken rissotto. Sandwiches, hot baguettes, jacket potatoes and ploughman's are also available, as is a good selection of real ales, many from Kent. Telephone: 01795 590088.

There are many pubs, cafés and restaurants in Faversham.

THE WALK

From the car park return to **North Lane**; then turn right by **Faversham Brewery**. After 150 yards, turn left into **Bridge Road** to cross **Faversham Creek**. Once over the water, turn immediately right by an information board to walk between a row of terraced houses called **Front Brents** and the creek. Where these houses end, keep straight on. The path then swings inland to skirt some newer houses. When the path ends at a road, go ahead for 30 yards to the end house and then turn right onto a stony path, part of the **Saxon Shore Way** long-distance footpath.

Where the path forks after 100 yards, keep right to walk alongside a wall around industrial units. Follow the wall to the right from its corner to regain the bank of the creek. Turn left along the bank. Reconstructed sailing barges can often be seen to the right, as well as other boats moored on the opposite bank by the **Oyster Bay House** warehouse. There is now a long stretch of the walk following the grassy bank above the creek, with a good view back to the impressive spire of Faversham's main church.

Look out for swans and other birds on the inland lagoon, while many species of gulls, ducks and waders, the colourful shelduck and oystercatchers, can be seen at the margins of the creek. I was lucky enough to see over ten little egrets when I did the walk. These elegant, pure-white birds now breed in the area, bringing an exotic touch to the marshy creeks. As you pass these marshy areas there are splashes of colour from specialized saltmarsh plants such as sea aster and golden samphire.

After 2 miles of walking on the bank of the creek you reach a group of buildings which includes the **Shipwright's Arms** pub and you can drop down from the bank to visit it.

Drive and Stroll

From the pub return to the bank and follow it as it bends left past a boatyard and a phalanx of moored yachts. Keep straight on as a narrow road goes off to the left, now with bushes between the path and the water. On reaching a road into a factory, keep straight ahead past another boatyard and follow the rough road alongside **Oare Creek**, with Oare church and village visible on the opposite bank. On the left is a large lagoon with cormorants, great crested grebes and other water-loving birds. After passing moored boats you reach a crossroads.

Turn left to walk alongside a road, initially past an industrial estate and then past **Mill House** where there is the tower of a disused windmill. Continue beside the road, with a tall hedge to your right and a lake hidden behind it, to reach a school. Keep straight on to the pretty church at **Davington**, founded in 1153, originally as part of a Benedictine priory. Keep straight ahead, with the tall wall of the churchyard on your right, to go downhill. After 100 yards, go left along narrow **Brent Lane**. To the right are views over the valley, once the site of gunpowder works, while on the left are some grand houses that once belonged to the officials who ran the works. At the bottom of the hill ignore a footpath going off to the right and continue along the road, with Faversham church spire visible ahead and less elegant industrial units on the left. At a T-junction turn right to cross **Faversham Creek** again, with a warehouse dating back to 1476 on the left. At the next T-junction, by **Shepherd Neame's brewery**, turn right and, shortly, left to the car park.

Places of Interest Nearby

Brogdale Horticultural Trust, south of the A2, houses the national fruit collection, the largest collection of fruit varieties in the world. There is also a restaurant, shop and plant centre. Telephone: 01795 535286.

14 Dering Wood, Pluckley

Looking towards Pluckley

The Walk 3 miles
Terrain Generally level on lanes and woodland paths
Map OS Explorer 137 Ashford (GR 898447)

How to get there

Pluckley is reached by B roads going south from the A20 at Charing or north from the A28 at Bethersden. The Woodland Trust reserve of Dering Wood is 1½ miles east of Pluckley on a B road. **Parking** At the Dering Wood car park. **Public transport** Pluckley station is 1¼ miles from the route.

Drive and Stroll

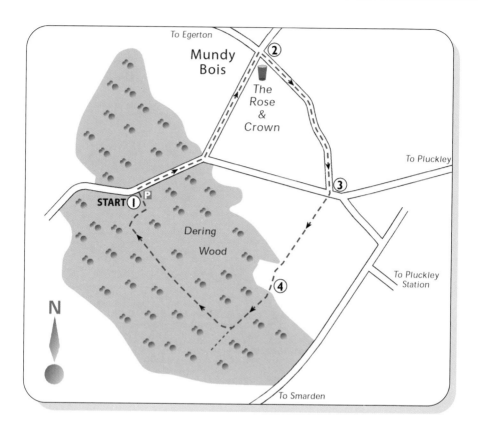

Introduction

Dering Wood, the base for this walk, is an area of ancient woodland, now owned by the Woodland Trust, and there is an opportunity to sample its many delights in the form of fine trees and colourful wild flowers and butterflies. (However, be warned that there are also some not-so-friendly mosquitoes in high summer.) Dering Wood appears in records dating back 1,000 years and was once part of the large estate owned by the Dering family. Much of the wood is mature hornbeam coppice: this tree produces a very hard wood which has been used for butchers' chopping blocks, mallets, spokes and cogwheels.

The first part of the walk takes you along lanes, the margins of which are also full of wild flowers, and past a good pub. As you continue there are spectacular views to the Greensand Ridge, with Pluckley village and church perched on it. The village has some interesting buildings and is reputed to be one of the most haunted places in the country. The final section of the walk is on field paths through flowery meadows and then back through the wood, carpeted with wood anemones and bluebells in spring.

The Rose and Crown

This pub at Mundy Bois is passed on the walk and provides a welcoming atmosphere in its bar area and the cosy candlelit, non-smoking dining room, while outside there is a patio and garden with a children's playground. The menu includes beef fillet gateau with a Stilton crust served with fondant potato and beef tomato in port wine jus, and baked sea bass with a creamy lemon and lime butter. Bar meals include local sausages, and there are salads, baguettes and sandwiches. Telephone: 01233 840393.

THE WALK

①

From the car park turn right out of the entrance and continue alongside the road; this can be busy, so it is safest to walk along the verge on the opposite side. After 400 yards, as the road bends right, go left on a lane and follow it for ½ mile. In summer there are creamy white flowers of meadowsweet and in the ditch on the right purple knapweed attracts meadow brown and gatekeeper butterflies.

②

At a crossroads turn right, soon to reach the **Rose and Crown** pub. This area is known as **Mundy Bois**, the name possibly originating from the time when French prisoners of war were exercised in the nearby woods (bois). The walk continues along the road – there can be quite a lot of traffic, so use the verge where

necessary, particularly on the blind bends.

As you walk there are fine views to the left, where Pluckley village and church can be seen perched on the Greensand Ridge, while in the hedges are occasional splashes of purple from the flowers of tufted vetch.

③

After ¾ mile you reach a T-junction. Cross with care to a footpath sign and stile hidden in the hedge to the left of the gateway to **Pinnock Lodge**; then proceed along the right edge of a field to a stile. Continue along the right edge of a longer field, which often has a herd of a pretty breed of cattle called British White, which originated in East Anglia and have black noses and ears. Pass a pond on your left; then, at the end of the fence on the right, 20 yards before the end of the field, go right over a stile at a marker post and then maintain your previous direction, now between fences. Continue ahead through a metal gate and along the right edge of a meadow, with flowers such as pink centaury and purple self-heal in summer, to reach another gate. Keep straight on for 20 yards to a footbridge and stile in trees; then go ahead between trees on the left and a fence on the right until a stile is reached.

Five yards on from the stile is a gate into the Woodland Trust reserve. Follow the path into the wood for 150 yards to a short marker post on the right with a red arrow on its far side. One option is to turn right here to follow a path with occasional marker posts back to the car park. However, to see more of the wood keep straight on at this post; then, after a few hundred yards, look for a marker post with an arrow and number 4 in red, alongside a post with a yellow band. Turn right here, soon to pass two benches

commemorating a golden jubilee, and continue along a grassy ride between trees.

There are patches of vivid purple flowers of rosebay willow-herb and yellow flowers of bird's-foot trefoil and spearwort. You may see butterflies such as speckled wood, and in June and July you may be lucky enough to see a white admiral, quite rare in Kent. This butterfly has striking black and white colouring and a soaring flight.

At the end of the ride, by a wooden bench donated by the Rotary Club, go slightly diagonally right at a marker post with red and blue arrows, to walk on a wide track through trees. At a cross-track with a marker post, turn left to reach the car park after a few yards. In this area you can see the wild honeysuckle on which the caterpillars of the white admiral feed.

Places of Interest Nearby

Godinton House and Gardens, 6 miles to the east, has lovely gardens and trees surrounding a Jacobean house. Telephone: 01233 620773.

15 | Boughton Lees

Rolling downland near Westwell

The Walk 5 miles
Terrain Mainly lanes and well-defined footpaths, some gentle climbs
Map OS Explorer 137 Ashford (GR 022473)

How to get there

Boughton Lees is on the A251 between Ashford and Challock. **Parking** Off the main road, alongside the green; please park with consideration. **Public transport** There are buses from Ashford and Faversham.

Drive and Stroll

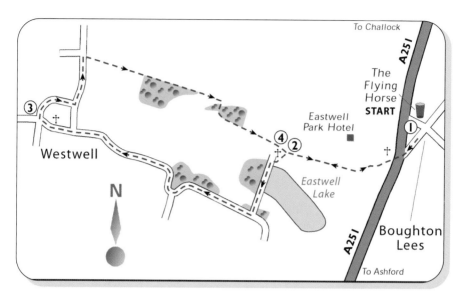

Introduction

As it winds through the lovely scenery of the North Downs, this walk takes you past several historical places. You pass Eastwell Park, an enormous mansion built in the Elizabethan style. In its grounds are impressive trees and a large lake that attracts many types of water birds. You also pass the atmospheric ruins of a church, in the graveyard of which lie the remains of a person reputed to be related to the Plantagenet kings. The route then follows quiet lanes to the tiny village of Westwell, with its watermill, manor house and old church, before returning through rolling downland to the large green and inn at Boughton Lees.

The Flying Horse

This inn stands beside the green at Boughton Lees, in a fine position overlooking the cricket matches played there in summer. It is an old pub with beams, stone-arched windows and a big inglenook fireplace. The pleasant bar area serves meals such as breaded scampi or plaice and chicken and bacon salad and offers a good choice of ales. There is also a separate restaurant, offering dishes such as chicken breast with tarragon and mushroom sauce and rack of lamb with redcurrant. A spacious garden, scented by roses in summer, makes a good place to sit in fine weather. Telephone: 01233 620914.

THE WALK

Walk past the war memorial on the edge of the green and cross the main road with care. Just to the left of **St Christopher's church** (built of white brick), go up the bank to an information board about the North Downs Way (NDW) long-distance footpath and go through a kissing gate next to it. Go slightly diagonally left through parkland. There are glimpses to the right of **Eastwell Park**, the manor house of the estate. The path goes through a kissing gate to a drive, along it for 30 yards and then through another gate on the left and diagonally left up a field to a marker post in a fence. Stay this side of the fence and walk alongside it to the right, later ignoring a stile in it, to reach a kissing gate where the fence ends. Keep straight on along a tarmac drive, soon with a large lake visible on the left and then a church ahead to the left.

After passing two lovely cedar trees and just after the driveway to a house on the left, leave the NDW by going left through a kissing gate hidden behind a laurel hedge and marked FP214. Go along the left edge of a small field and then enter the churchyard through a gate. Go diagonally right, past the remains of the church, to a lane.

The watermill at Westwell

St Mary's churchyard has a stone tablet to mark the burial place of Richard Plantagenet, the illegitimate son of Richard III. He fled to Kent after his father was killed and lived in semi-secrecy on the Eastwell Park estate until his death in 1550.

Turn left along the lane. Continue along the lane to a T-junction and turn right into another lane. After ½ mile keep straight on where a lane goes off left, and, ¾ mile further on, keep straight on when another lane goes off right. Soon pass a mill house. You are now in the small village of **Westwell** and pass a manor house, with a huge barn across the road from it, and then the historic church.

Drive and Stroll

On reaching a crossroads, there is **the Wheel** pub on the left if you require refreshment, but the walk goes right, along **Gold Hill**, which bends right to a T-junction. Turn left here to go uphill on a lane, under overhanging trees. At the top of the hill, where a lane goes off left, turn right at a footpath sign to get back on the NDW and cross a stile. Go sharp left along the field edge for 80 yards; then turn right on a wide track between fields. Keep ahead on the track, for about a mile until you reach a 'No Entry to the Public' sign. Turn right here at a marker post to walk through a gap in the belt of trees for 100 yards; then go left at a footpath sign to walk alongside a wood on the left. At the corner of the wood and fence keep straight on across a field to a stile and then go ahead along a tarmac drive.

You are now back near the ruined church and must do the outward journey in reverse to return to the start. Keep ahead along the drive until you reach a T-junction with another drive; then go straight on through a kissing gate. Keep alongside the fence and after passing a horse chestnut tree reach a marker post in the fence. From there go diagonally left down the field to a gate; turn right along the drive for 30 yards to another gate on the left; and then go diagonally left across grass to return to the main road and green at **Boughton Lees**.

Places of Interest Nearby

Beech Court Gardens, near Challock, contain a superb collection of trees, shrubs, roses and other flowers. Plants are available for purchase, as are refreshments. Telephone: 01233 740735.

16 | Dymchurch

The beach at Dymchurch

The Walk 5¼ or 6 miles
Terrain Level, on concrete apron, lanes and field paths
Map OS Explorer 125 Romney Marsh (GR 101290)

How to get there

Dymchurch is on the A259 between New Romney and Hythe. **Parking** At the pay and display car park at the southern end of the village, next to a Martello tower. **Public transport** Dymchurch can be reached by bus from Folkestone and Hythe.

Drive and Stroll

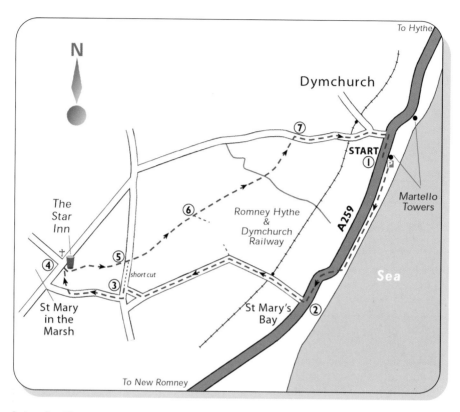

Introduction

This is one of the longer walks in the book, but has the advantage of being flat. It starts on the coast near a Martello tower, a fortification dating back to Napoleonic times, and there is a bracing stretch along the promenade with views to Dungeness ahead and to Folkestone to the rear. There is also the opportunity to do some beachcombing for shells or spot seabirds and waders. The route then goes inland on lanes, with the chance to visit a pub near an ancient church. The return journey samples the unique atmosphere of Romney Marsh as you walk over former marshland, using footbridges to cross the numerous drainage ditches. The reed-filled ditches are home to water-loving plants and birds, while the reclaimed fields support flocks of the local breed of sheep. The final section back into Dymchurch crosses a famous narrow-gauge railway and passes some lovely old cottages.

The Star Inn

This inn can be found opposite the church in the hamlet of St Mary in the Marsh. The building dates from 1476, when it was a thatched farm cottage; it is now a relaxed, down-to-earth pub. The menu includes chilli con carne, cod and chips and cream cheese and broccoli bake, and sandwiches, toasted sandwiches and ploughman's are also available. Telephone: 01797 362139.

There are also pubs and cafés in Dymchurch.

THE WALK

###

From the car park, walk up the steps to the concrete promenade and turn right. As you walk along the prom (or the beach below) you can see Dungeness power station in the distance ahead. Looking back you can see along the coast to Hythe and Folkestone. There are plenty of shells to find on the beach and you may see wading birds such as sanderling and oystercatcher on the edge of the water. After ¾ mile, continue past another pay and display car park behind the sea wall at **St Mary's Bay**. Then, about 300 yards further on, as the main road bends away from the wall to the right, go through a gap in the wall and across tarmac to the road. Cross with care and turn left on the path alongside the road.

###

Turn right along **Jefferstone Road** (signed to the village hall and St Mary in the Marsh). Go past the **Bailiff's Sergeant** pub and the tracks of the Romney, Hythe and Dymchurch miniature steam railway, and continue to walk along the lane as it bends left after a group of bungalows. Take care, as there is no footpath now and although the lane is fairly quiet there are several bends. About ¾ mile past the bungalows, turn right along another lane, signed to Newchurch, to reach a T-junction by **Ivy House**.

###

(For the shorter walk turn right here for ¼ mile, and, just past a house, turn right on a footpath and then follow the instructions from point 5.) For the extra one-mile loop to the pub, turn left for 200 yards and then right on a lane signed to St Mary in the Marsh. After 400 yards, just after the lane crosses a ditch, look for a footpath sign hidden in a hawthorn bush on the right and go through a gap in the hedge. The path across the field may not be clear, but go in a diagonal, aiming for the church ahead. (The alternative to crossing the field is to continue along the lane to a T-junction and then turn right to the church.) At the far right corner of the field, near the church, go through a gate to a road; the pub is immediately to the right, opposite the church. **St Mary's church** is Norman, with a heavily buttressed west tower.

In the churchyard is the grave of Edith Nesbit, author of The Railway Children.

From the pub retrace your steps through the gate and keep to the left edge of the field to the end of the pub's garden. Then go diagonally left, aiming for the right end of houses jutting out into the field. At the end of a tall coniferous hedge in the garden of the end house, go sharp right across the field to cross a footbridge over a ditch. Continue slightly diagonally left across the next field, aiming several hundred yards left of a white house at the far end, to reach a yellow-painted pole in a hedge. From the gap in this hedge, continue slightly diagonally left towards the left telegraph pole of several at the far side of the field, about 200 yards to the right of a corrugated barn. Cross a footbridge to a road.

Go straight across the road (or turn right off it if you have omitted the pub loop) to a marker post and a footbridge; then keep ahead on a grassy path between fields. Continue ahead, now with a willow hedge and ditch on your right and a view ahead to the ridge above

Hythe. Where the hedge ends, go left for 10 yards to cross another footbridge; then go straight ahead, keeping straight on when the ditch to your right bends away right after 100 yards. Cross a footbridge between two prominent hawthorn bushes and continue ahead, keeping parallel with, and about 20 yards left of, a sparse line of bushes, to reach a stile next to a gateway and small pond.

The path divides here: ignore the path going off to the right and keep straight ahead across a large field towards a phone mast in the middle distance. At the far end of the field, cross a footbridge over a reed-filled ditch and then go slightly diagonally right over another field to reach a wider ditch. Turn right and keep alongside it for a short distance before crossing it on a footbridge. Ahead is a line of telegraph poles, but you need to go slightly diagonally right away from them to a yellow-banded marker post at the corner of a ditch. Continue ahead, alongside the ditch, to a road.

Turn right along the road, soon passing a caravan park and later crossing the miniature railway and a wide dyke. Go past some attractive white-boarded cottages to reach a T-junction and then turn right for a few yards to return to the car park and **Martello tower**.

A line of 103 towers was built along the south coast in 1804–5 to defend England in the event of a French invasion. They were called Martello towers after a similar fortification at Mortella in Corsica. The walls are 13 feet thick on the seaward side to withstand bombardment from ships, and the gun mounted on the flat roof could fire a cannon ball for 1,000 yards.

Places of Interest Nearby

The Romney, Hythe and Dymchurch Railway is a miniature-gauge railway, opened in 1927, which is operated by steam trains over a 14-mile track across Romney Marsh. Telephone: 01797 362353.

The Romney Marsh Visitor Centre, on the A259 south of Dymchurch, is operated by Kent Wildlife Trust and has exhibitions on natural history, local history and other features of the area. Telephone: 01797 369487.

17 Wickhambreaux

A thatched house in Wickhambreaux

The Walk 3¾ miles
Terrain Generally level, on lanes and field paths
Map OS Explorer 150 Canterbury and the Isle of Thanet (GR 221587)

How to get there

Wickhambreaux is reached by a minor road going north from the A257 at Littlebourne, between Canterbury and Wingham. **Parking** There is limited parking around the green at Wickhambreaux. An alternative is the car park at the nature reserve in Stodmarsh, ¼ mile off the route (GR 221609). **Public transport** Not practicable

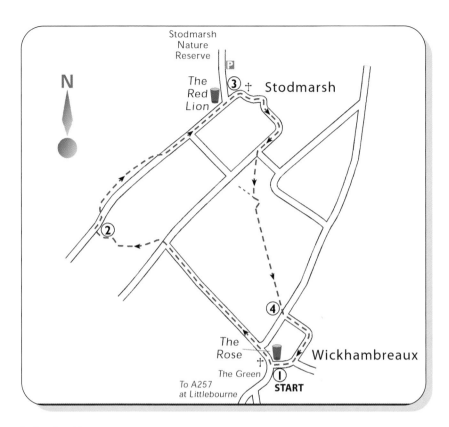

Introduction

Starting in the village of Wickhambreaux, at the picturesque green surrounded by church, manor house, restored watermill and pub, the walk goes via lanes and field paths to Stodmarsh. Here you may want to make a short diversion to visit the national nature reserve, renowned for the birds that visit the flooded pits and reed beds. The village also has a pub and a lovely Norman church. The return is via lanes and fields of strawberries.

The Rose

This pub is in a delightful situation opposite the green in the village of Wickhambreaux. The building dates from the 14th century, and the interior of stripped brick, beams and panelling reflects its age. There is also a big fireplace which houses a welcoming log fire in winter and a separate non-smoking restaurant. Selections from the menu are griddled lamb leg steak in redcurrant and Stilton sauce and pan-grilled chicken breast in a white wine and cream sauce. There are children's and vegetarian meals, and ploughman's, salads, jacket potatoes, baguettes and sandwiches are also served. Telephone: 01227 721753.

THE WALK

Facing the green and church, go right along the road past the **Old Rectory** and straight ahead along **Wickham Court Road**. This narrow lane is lined by tall poplars on the right, and there are distant views over the hedge on the left. At a T-junction with another road after ⅔ mile, go straight across and over a stile to the right of a metal gate. Go slightly diagonally left for 70 yards; then go left through a gateway just past an oak tree and walk down a long, narrow field with a line of ash and other trees on the left. Head for the far right corner at the end of the field to cross a stile and footbridge. Then bear diagonally left for 30 yards to cross two more stiles in quick succession. From the second, turn sharp right along the right edge of a field beside a wire fence with conifers behind to reach a stile in the corner. Continue ahead on a path between wire garden fences to a road.

Turn right to follow the road round a bend. Then either continue along the road, or, to reduce road walking, cross a stile on the left, signed Stour Valley Walk, and turn right to walk parallel to the road along a field. If taking the latter option, leave the field over a stile next to a green gate to get back onto the road. Whichever route you choose for this stretch, there are views along the Stour Valley on the left. Passing an old house and a converted barn, continue along the road to reach the village of **Stodmarsh** and an alternative pub stop at the **Red Lion**.

The national nature reserve and car park at Stodmarsh are along the lane to the left here. The nature reserve has reed beds, which are home to reed and sedge warblers, bearded tits, reed buntings and the rare bittern, while the wet areas attract many species of waders and waterfowl, and marsh and hen harriers search for prey.

The walk, however, continues along the road, bending right past the picturesque Norman church. The small, simple church of **St Mary's** in **Stodmarsh** was built in the 12th and 13th centuries. On the south doorway are crosses carved by knights on their way to the crusades. Continue along the lane for ½ mile, through a series of bends, until you reach a tiny triangular green where another lane goes off left. Here go diagonally left at a footpath sign to cross a long field. At its end, turn left at a marker post to walk on the far side of a wire fence and along the left edge of a field, with a windbreak of alder trees on the left. When I did the walk the field had beds of strawberry plants growing under plastic tunnels. After 250 yards, turn right at the end of the field onto a track in front of another windbreak to reach a rough farm road after 100 yards. Turn left on this road as it goes between fields; then, on reaching the farm buildings, go straight across the yard to a kissing gate and maintain direction over a small field to a gate to a road. Ahead on the left is a large thatched house.

④

Go straight across the road and ahead along a narrow lane with the unusual name of **The List**. Follow it as it bends right to go through **Wickhambreaux** village and bring you back to the green. On the way you will see a mixture of architecture including weatherboarded and thatched cottages and a converted oast house. **St Andrew's** church by the green dates from the 14th century, but was restored in the 19th century. It has a lovely stained-glass window designed by Baron Arild Rosenkrantz in 1896.

Places of Interest Nearby

Wingham Wildlife Park, along the A257 to the east, has a wide variety of animals and birds, plus an adventure playground. Telephone: 01227 722053.

Howletts Wild Animal Park, 3 miles south-west of Wickhambreaux at Bekesbourne, has a large group of gorillas, in addition to tigers, elephants and many other animals. Telephone: 09068 800605.

18 Barham

The village of Barham

The Walk 4½ or 5 miles
Terrain Undulating on lanes and field paths.
Map OS Explorer 138 Dover and Folkestone (GR 207501)

How to get there

How to get there Barham is reached on minor roads, signed from the A2 south of Canterbury and Bridge. **Parking** Travelling south on the road into the village, turn left into The Street and park beside the village green or nearby in the village. **Public transport** Buses run to Barham from Canterbury.

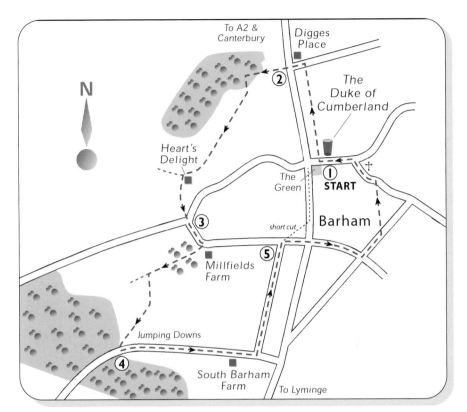

Introduction

The Elham Valley, where this walk is based, has some of the loveliest countryside in Kent. The stream that runs through the valley, the Nailbourne, can dry up for several years and then start running again. On the chalk sides of the valley are many woods, and a small area of restored grassland is rich in downland flowers. The hills here have been used by armies since Roman times and there is further historical interest in the ancient church and picturesque old houses in the village of Barham, which is the base for this walk. Even some of the hedges on the route are old, the evidence for this being the number of species of shrubs and trees they contain.

The Duke of Cumberland

Situated in Barham, this is a traditional village pub, with attractive scrubbed pine tables in the bar area and a separate restaurant. There is also seating in a patio garden. The meals include grilled trout with almonds and pan-fried salmon with cajun spices. Omelettes, sandwiches and ploughman's are also available, and there is a children's menu. A choice of several ales is on offer. Telephone: 01227 831396.

THE WALK

Opposite the corner of the green nearest the pub, take a gravel track at a footpath sign next to a white bungalow called **Whitebeams**. Continue ahead to the left of a garden fence to cross a stile and go along the left edge of a field to another stile. Go straight on along the right edge of the next field to a stile and then keep ahead across a field, aiming for the corner of a fence jutting out into the field on the right. Continue ahead alongside the fence, passing a large Georgian house to reach a lane. Turn left to pass **Digges Place**, an impressive building dating from the 17th century, and a ford over the Nailbourne stream, often dry, and reach a busy road.

Cross with care to a bridleway sign and go straight ahead on a track between fields. As the track bends right at the top of the slope, go straight on through a pedestrian gate next to a larger gate and onto a path to the left of a wood. Then go through trees for 150 yards to a stony cross-track. Turn left on this track, which is part of the **Elham**

Valley Way long-distance footpath. The track goes through trees and then between hedges, which are very old, as evidenced by the diversity of species they contain, including hazel, dogwood, spindle, blackthorn, field maple and wild privet. They are draped with traveller's joy, bryony and honeysuckle, and there are flowers like yarrow, bedstraw and mallow at their base. Where the track forks, keep right to pass a pear orchard. The group of dwellings here rejoices in the name of **Heart's Delight** and includes a Tudor farmhouse. Keep straight on where a track goes off right, to reach a large white-painted house with oasts at the rear. Alongside this house, take the lower of two parallel tracks to go alongside a black-boarded barn. Where this concrete track bends left, go straight ahead on a grassy track for 100 yards; then keep right of a metal gate to go ahead on a path between a line of oak trees on the right and a fence. Cross a stile and then go slightly diagonally left up a field with fine views behind. Walk through a belt of trees to a stile next to a metal gate and onto a lane at **Railway Hill**, a reminder of the railway that used to run along the valley.

The path over the downs

Go straight across and along the lane opposite. Where the lane bends sharp left after 300 yards, turn right in front of the entrance to **Millfields Farm** to go on an earth track through trees. When the track bends left after about 400 yards, keep straight ahead on a narrower track, which can be muddy. On emerging from the trees, keep ahead along the right edge of a field, and after 400 yards go diagonally left at a marker post to cross the field to a stile. Maintain direction across the next field to a gate in a gap in the trees in the bottom corner. With good views along the valley to the left, continue downhill alongside a fence and reach a lane.

You are allowed to walk in the woods to the right here, owned by Forest Enterprise, but the walk continues to the left along the lane.

On the left is Jumping Downs, an area of restored chalk grassland now designated a local nature reserve. It is well worth a short diversion into the reserve in summer to view the rich mixture of wild flowers, including bee and pyramidal orchids, rockrose and horseshoe vetch, and butterflies such as the marbled white, which has a lovely black and white chequered pattern.

Continue down the lane, now between hedges, and pass the buildings and milking parlour of **South Barham Farm**. Then, 200 yards past the farm and 100 yards before a junction with a busy road, turn left along a narrow lane and follow it for ¾ mile back to the outskirts of **Barham**.

When the lane reaches a T-junction you have a choice of routes. For the shorter distance back to the start, go straight ahead past another ford and along a tarmac path called **The Causeway** to reach the main road through the village. Turn left and keep alongside it for ¼ mile to return to the village green and pub. For a longer walk, adding ½ mile, to view the church and older part of Barham, turn right along the road by the ford, passing attractive cottages before you reach the main street. Go straight across with care and along narrow **Brickfield Road** opposite. At a crossroads turn left; then, just past the drive to 'Aylets', go left over a stile at a footpath sign and up a bank. Continue across a field, aiming for the left end of a line of trees extending into the field from the right. The impressive spire of **Barham church** comes into view ahead, while looking back there are superb views along the Elham Valley and to the hills where the Britons encountered Caesar's Romans. Keep ahead over two stiles and go alongside a graveyard to a lane near the church. Turn left to follow the lane as it bends past the church, the manor house of **Barham Court** and some lovely cottages, and then goes downhill to reach the pub and green. Barham church has a tower of the 12th or early 13th century. One wing of the 17th-century house survives; the rest was rebuilt in 1735 and then enlarged by Sir Edwin Lutyens in 1911.

Places of Interest Nearby

Higham Park, just south of Bridge, is a beautiful mansion with lovely Italianate gardens and a tea lawn. Telephone: 01227 830830.

Elham Valley Vineyard is at Breach, just south of Barham, and has wines to sample. There is also a pottery and gift shop. Telephone: 01227 831266.

19 | Kearsney

The Alkham valley near Kearsney

The Walk 3 or 5 miles
Terrain Some steep climbs and descents, some of which can be slippery and muddy after wet weather. It is necessary to have a reasonable level of fitness and suitable footwear.
Map OS Explorer 138 Dover, Folkestone and Hythe (GR 287438)

How to get there

Kearsney is ½ mile off the A256, 2 miles north-west of Dover. It can also be reached from the A2 by turning off at Whitfield onto the A256. Turn west off the A256 and follow the signs for Kearsney Abbey. **Parking** There are car parks at the abbey and 200 yards west at Russell Gardens. **Public transport** Kearsney railway station is ¼ mile from the start.

Drive and Stroll

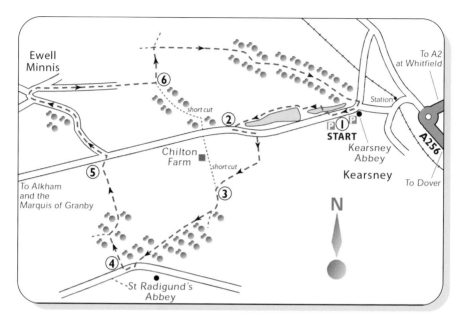

Introduction

Starting at some lovely public gardens just outside Dover, this walk goes through some of the most beautiful countryside in Kent. The route goes along both sides of a deep valley, providing wonderful views. Apart from the lovely scenery, there are colourful wild flowers and butterflies and woods with a wide diversity of trees.

Kearsney Abbey, near the start of the walk, was never a real abbey; it was a gothic-style mansion with 15 bedrooms, built in 1822. Sadly, the house succumbed to dry rot and was demolished in 1959, except for the billiard room, which is now the café. The 25 acres of grounds have been converted to a lovely park by Dover Council. A short extension to the walk, however, offers the opportunity to view the remains of a real abbey.

The Marquis of Granby

This pub at Alkham, 2 miles west of Kearsney, is set in a lovely position in the valley, with the village church behind it. It dates from 1810 and has pleasant bar areas and a beamed restaurant. There is also a garden. As it is so close to the south coast ports, it is not surprising that there is an emphasis on fish, including Dover and lemon sole and sea bass, or you could tackle the fisherman's platter of scampi, plaice, scallops and haddock, preferably after the walk! Also available are sandwiches, hot and cold baguettes, jacket potatoes and ploughman's, plus a good choice of ales. Telephone: 01304 822945.

There is a café at **Kearsney Abbey**, serving snacks and hot meals in the ornate surroundings of the old billiard room of the mansion.

THE WALK

If parked near the café at Kearsney Abbey, go out of the entrance, turn left and walk beside the road for 200 yards then cross to the opposite side. (If you are in the Russell Gardens car park, cross the main road from the entrance.) Go through a pedestrian gate into the gardens and turn left. After 30 yards, turn right over a pagoda-style footbridge and immediately left onto a tarmac path alongside an ornamental lake. Keep ahead past a similar footbridge and a playground and alongside a stream on the left; then cross a footbridge to the left of a flint cottage. After 40 yards, bear right over a bridge and then turn immediately left to walk alongside a large lake on the left, home to swans and coot. To the right is a large colonial-style house, built in 1825, while nearby there used to be a paper mill dating from 1794. Continue between the lake and a bank with trees and where the lake ends keep ahead on the raised path on the right, soon on a narrower path through trees to a pedestrian gate. Take great care before going through it, as it leads straight onto a busy road.

Cross the road with care and turn left along the edge of it for 300 yards before going right at a bridleway sign. Walk up the left edge of a field, keeping straight on when the fence on the left ends. At the top of the field go through a metal gate and then turn sharp right to walk alongside a fence on the right, with superb views along the valley. At the end of the long field go ahead, through a metal gate to a cross-track.

For the shorter walk, turn right on the track to go downhill; then go through farm buildings to a road. Go straight across to a track opposite, into trees and uphill. Follow the track as it bends left and then goes through a wood and between fields to reach an open area with an isolated tree. Here go over a stile in the fence opposite and follow the instructions from point 6.

For the longer walk, turn left on the track and after 100 yards keep ahead alongside the wood on the left rather than through a gate into it. After ½ mile, with downland flowers and blue butterflies on the fringe of the wood, go through a metal gate and ahead on a track

Drive and Stroll

through trees, with hart's-tongue ferns growing beneath. On reaching a lane on a bend, go right for 30 yards; then the walk continues by turning right on an unmarked track into a wood.

At this point, you may wish to consider a short extension of ⅔ mile to see the remains of a real abbey. Continue along the lane for 100 yards and then go left over a stile and slightly diagonally left across a field. Go through a metal gate and maintain direction across a smaller field to reach the remains of **St Radigund's Abbey**. It is private, but by going left on the tarmac road in front of it, a public footpath, you can view the best-preserved part of the ruins.

The abbey was founded in the late 12th century, but had fallen into disrepair by the 1500s.

Retrace your steps to the lane and the track into the wood.

The track goes through the edge of the wood, between fields and then into another wood, going downhill

under trees. At a fork in the track by a marker post, turn right to soon go more steeply downhill through trees on a path that can be muddy and slippery. Later there is a superb view along the valley on the left to the village of **Alkham**. Continue downhill between hedges and trees and then go ahead on a track past houses to a road.

Cross with care and go up **Wolverton Hill** opposite, where the lane climbs quite steeply for ½ mile. Continue past **Green Lane** where it goes off left and then turn right by a postbox and phone box to go along **Newcastle Lane** for 200 yards. Then take the right fork to continue along the narrow **Red Barn Lane**. Where this lane ends, keep ahead on a track between hedges to reach an open area with an isolated tree and, in the fence on the left, a stile.

Cross the stile. You are now on land belonging to the Ministry of Defence and must keep to the designated footpaths. Go slightly diagonally right across the field to a tall hedge at the far end. Don't go through a gate or a

Russell Gardens

gap in the hedge but turn right on the near side to walk alongside the hedge and some oak trees. At the end of the long field, go through a gap in blackthorn scrub and through a gate. Then go ahead on a track through trees, which after about 300 yards bends right and passes two white houses. Remain on the track as it bends right again and goes steeply downhill under trees, later becoming a tarmac road. On reaching a main road, turn right for a short distance to the car parks on the opposite side.

20 Walmer

The cliffs at Kingsdown

The Walk 2¾ miles
Terrain Gently undulating on field paths, then level on a tarmac path
Map OS Explorer 138 Dover, Folkestone and Hythe (GR 378503)

How to get there

Walmer is on the A258 between Dover and Deal. Travelling north turn right from the A258 in Walmer, following the signs for Walmer Castle. **Parking** In the car park almost opposite the castle entrance. **Public transport** Walmer railway station is 1 mile from the start of the walk.

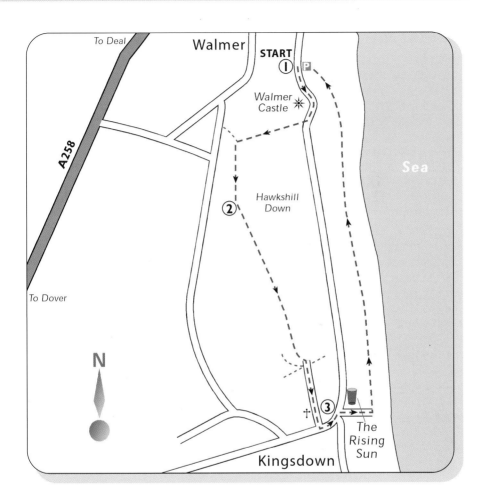

Introduction

This walk provides the opportunity to get some bracing sea air and visit a picturesque castle with beautiful gardens. The route takes you past the grounds of Walmer Castle, then over higher ground with excellent sea views. You can watch the ferries and other boats in the busy English Channel and on a clear day you can spy the coast of France. As you return to the sea front at Kingsdown, there are views of white cliffs and a choice of pubs. Your return to Walmer goes beside the shingle beach, home to specialized wild flowers. Ahead there are views to Deal and Pegwell Bay.

Drive and Stroll

The Rising Sun

This pub at Kingsdown is situated in a pretty clapboard cottage, built in 1692. It has pleasant eating areas both inside and out. As befits the pub's proximity to the sea, its menu includes lemon sole stuffed with crab in a seafood sauce as well as other non-fish selections such as steak and stout pie. There are also jacket potatoes, salads and sandwiches, and a children's menu. Telephone: 01304 373983.

If you visit the castle at Walmer, there is a tearoom there.

THE WALK

###

Facing the castle, go left from the car park and walk alongside the road to pass the castle. Take care as you go round the bend and cross the road to a footpath at the end of the metal fence around the castle grounds. The path goes inland from the road, with a tall brick wall to the right and gardens on the left. After ¼ mile it opens out at a grassy area. Here you go left on a path at the edge of longer grass to walk parallel to a hedge on the left, through which there are views to the sea.

On the right there is a windmill visible in the distance and the meadow alongside you has colourful wild flowers such as red clover and wild carrot, attracting butterflies and other insects in summer.

The path goes past two wooden seats to reach a cross path near a third seat.

###

Go diagonally left on a narrow stony path, passing a small memorial to airmen who were stationed at an aerodrome on these cliffs and died in the First World War. Ignore a footpath going off left and continue ahead between hedges, with more sea views to the left. After a while, the path opens out, with views ahead over the bay to distant cliffs. Continue ahead to cross a field; where the path forks at the end, take the left fork. Go straight across a drive and ahead on a path between gardens to reach a cross path. Here go diagonally left for 20 yards to another cross path. Go straight across it and up a slope for 10 yards, walking between two wooden posts to reach the end of a residential road. Keep straight on along the road, passing a church and reaching a T-junction with another road. This road is busy; so take care as you cross and turn left for 20 yards to a bend.

###

The **Rising Sun** pub is 70 yards to the left here, but the walk goes straight on as the road bends left. Cross a minor road and go ahead on a gravel road (**South Road**) and past

Walmer Castle

a row of cottages to the sea front. To the right are views to white cliffs, and on a clear day the coast of France can be seen. Turn left on a road past another pub, the **Zetland Arms**, and, where this road ends, keep ahead on a path between houses and the shingle beach. The tarmac path is now followed back to **Walmer**, with views to Deal and Pegwell Bay ahead.

Although it makes for harder

walking, it is worth some excursions along the shingle, where there are specialized maritime plants such as yellow horned-poppy and sea cabbage and where patches of red valerian attract butterflies such as painted ladies and red admirals that have flown over from continental Europe.

Where the houses end keep ahead on the tarmac path, soon to reach the castle and car park.

Places of Interest Nearby

Walmer Castle (English Heritage) is a coastal fort dating from the time of Henry VIII. It is the country residence of the Lord Warden of the Cinque Ports, two of the most famous people to hold this title having been the Duke of Wellington and Queen Elizabeth the Queen Mother. There are lovely gardens, a tearoom and gift shop. Telephone: 01304 364288.